INVITATION TO THE SOCIOLOGY OF RELIGION

PHIL ZUCKERMAN

D0103240

Routledge

NEW YORK AND LONDON

Published in 2003 by
Routledge
29 West 35th Street
New York, NY 10001
www.routledge-ny.com

Published in Great Britain by
Routledge
11 New Fetter Lane
London EC4P 4EE
www.routledge.co.uk

Routledge is an imprint of the Taylor & Francis Group.

Library of Congress Cataloging-in-Publication Data

Zuckerman, Phil.
    Invitation to the sociology of religion / Phil Zuckerman.
        p. cm.
Includes bibliographical references and index.
    ISBN 0-415-94125-3 (alk. paper) — ISBN 0-415-94126-1 (pbk. : alk. paper)
    1. Religion and sociology.   I. Title.
    BL60.Z83 2003
    306.6—dc21
                                                                    2003007398

Sociological jargon is usually filled with latinized concepts and complicated sentence structures. It is as if the use of ordinary words and sentences might decrease the trust in arguments and reasoning. I detest that tradition. So little of the sociology I am fond of needs technical terms and ornate sentences. I write with my "favourite aunts" in mind, fantasy figures of ordinary people, sufficiently fond of me to give the text a try, but not to the extent of using terms and sentences made complicated to look scientific.

—*Nils Christie*

CONTENTS

ACKNOWLEDGMENTS

I would like to thank my student research assistants, Gayla Hamik-Beckley and Shana Doerr. Additional thanks and gratitude to my friends and colleagues for their encouragement and scholarly advice: Benton Johnson, Joseph Bryant, Mark Shibley, Peter Nardi, Jill Brazier, and Amatzya Mezahav. I would also like to express my deep appreciation to Nick Street, who first believed in and supported this project. Sincere thankfulness and tremendous appreciation for hard work and insightful editing to Damian Treffs, Gilad Foss, and everyone else at Routledge. My ultimate thanks and gratitude to my father, Marvin Zuckerman, and especially my wife, Stacy Elliott, for crucial input, critical intellectual challenges, and personal inspiration. Finally, love to Ruby Pandora Natya and Flora Fredrika Delphina.

INTRODUCTION

Some of my best friends are religious. So are some of my closest relatives. So are most of my neighbors. The teachers and secretaries at my daughter's nursery school are religious, as well as the two brothers from Egypt who own and run my favorite pizza place. My mechanic is religious. So is my president. Some days it feels like the whole world is religious.

Whenever I drive anywhere, I can't help but notice the plethora of bumper stickers telling me about Jesus' love or God's blessings. Sometimes an occasional billboard along the freeway will echo their assertions. Whenever I turn on the little television attached to the jogging treadmill at the gym where I work out, I am entertained by Christian rock videos or informed by Christian news broadcasts. Whenever I walk into the chain bookstores at the nearby mall, I am greeted by rows and rows of religious best-sellers, from Armageddon-Apocalyptic serials to New Age spiritual advice, from the benefits of Zen meditation to the practical wisdom of the Cabala.

When I open my newspaper every morning, I am regularly confronted with religious matters, from controversies over priestly sexual abuse and child molestation in the Catholic Church to Falun Gong members meditating in Chinese prisons. Lately there's been a lot in the newspapers about a California federal appeals court ruling that the Pledge of Allegiance violates the Constitution with its reference to God—a ruling which the Congress, the Senate, and the president have denounced. In November 2002, hundreds of people in Kaduna, Nigeria, were killed and injured in rioting that erupted when a local newspaper questioned Muslim opposition to the Miss World beauty pageant. Other current religious issues permeating the news include religious/ethnic conflicts in Kashmir, Sudan, Egypt, Northern Ireland, Indonesia, Sri Lanka, Macedonia, Mexico, and Israel-Palestine.

1

And ever since September 11, religion has been a constant media staple, with regular stories on religious fundamentalism, the efficacy of prayer, God's wrath, End-Times prophecy, and so on.

The other night, my mother-in-law talked to me for over an hour about her worries concerning whether or not her daughter (my wife) would be able to cash in on her generous life insurance policy after the rapture—which she is sure will happen any day now. Last week, while standing in line at the grocery store, I noticed that the cover of *Newsweek* was about Heaven. A few months earlier the cover story was about God. And a few weeks ago, *Time* ran a cover story on the Apocalypse. And as I sit here writing this paragraph in my office of very liberal, extremely progressive, and ostensibly secular Pitzer College—the college which *The Princeton Review* website ranks fourth in the nation for "ignoring God on a regular basis"—I realize that among my colleagues with whom I share this hallway, one is a regularly meditating Buddhist, one is a Hindu who has been enthusiastically sharing her revelations with me from her recent study of the Bhagavad-Gita, and one is a self-described "pagan pantheist" who claims to be very spiritually connected with Earth. I'm not sure that any of my colleagues would actually label themselves "religious." For some, the term "religious" is synonymous with dogmatic, fundamentalist, unquestioning, or obedient (Zinnbauer et al. 1997). Like many of my friends (and especially my students), my colleagues would probably prefer to describe themselves as "spiritual"—a term which seems to imply a reluctance to belong to a specific religious movement or to accept a specific set of traditional beliefs, while at the same time maintaining a sincere openness to the sacred, a desire to connect to something bigger than ourselves, a willingness to admit that there is more to this life than that which can be rationally understood or empirically explained (see Marler and Hadaway 2002; Yip 2002; Fuller 2001). But whether they prefer the label "religious" or "spiritual," I find myself surrounded by people who certainly would not be described as irreligious, atheist, or secular.

The glaring truth is that despite the confident predictions of some of the most prominent European social theorists of the nineteenth century, religion hasn't died. Religion has not declined in the wake of the Enlightenment and the advances of science. Modernity has not bred a widespread, universal skepticism. With the glaring and note-worthy exception of selected countries in Western Europe (Bruce 2001; Grotenhuis and Scheepers 2001; Palm and Trost 2000; Davie 1999), most of the world is actually "bubbling with religious passions," to quote Peter Berger (2001). Religion not only persists, but as Batson, Schoenrader, and Ventis (1993, 4) observe, it provides for literally millions of people "the most significant, most joyful, the most meaningful moments of their lives." Additionally, tens of thousands of religious individuals and organizations are at the forefront of sustained attempts to alleviate human suffering around the world: feeding the hungry, sheltering the homeless, tending to the sick, caring for the orphaned, and the like. Yes, religion is very much alive and thriving on planet Earth—especially here in the United States (Greeley 1991). According to the research of Finke and Stark (1992), a greater proportion of Americans are church members today than at any other time in our country's history. A 2002 international survey conducted by the Pew Research Center for the People and Press found that 59 percent of Americans considered religion "very important" in their lives, compared with only 11 percent of respondents in France, 12 percent in Japan, 25 percent in South Korea, 27 percent in Italy, and 30 percent in Canada. Robert Fuller (2001, 1) has recently described the United States as "arguably the most religious nation on earth." Robert Putnam (2000, 65) concurs, characterizing the United States as one of the most religiously observant, God-believing, fundamentalist, and spiritually active countries in all Christendom.

Consider:

- 96 percent of Americans profess a belief in God, a percentage that has held steady for over fifty years.[1]
- One out of every three Americans claims to be a "born again" Christian.
- One out of every three Americans believes that the Bible "is the actual word of God and is to be taken literally, word for word."
- 68 percent of Americans believe in The Devil (Kristof 2003).

Of course, being an agnostic, I sometimes feel, well, taken aback by it all. Some days I am intrigued and enthralled by all the religion around me. Other days, I'm concerned. Or envious. Or suspicious. Or amused. Or daunted. Or curious. So much faith. So many houses of worship. So many people committing their lives to various gods and goddesses, engaging in extensive rituals, celebrating solemn or garish holy days, donating time and money to various congregations and organizations. So many people seemingly comforted by a confident belief in religious answers concerning life's deepest mysteries.

Take the mystery of death. I personally have absolutely no idea what happens when you die. But a lot of people do. I remember seeing this one particular commercial on television a few years ago when I was living in Eugene, Oregon. I was watching *Seinfeld* reruns late at night, and it was during the commercial break. There was a commercial for shampoo and then another one for a local car dealer and then came a commercial concerning the mystery of death. It began on an unambiguously somber note: dreary, melancholic music played while there were obscure images of a dark suit, a white hand, a leather shoe being polished, and then it quickly became apparent that what was being shown was actually a corpse being clothed, cleaned, and prepared for a funeral. Then came the frightening climax of the commercial: from the corpse's point of view we see the casket lid come closing over us and shutting with a dull thud. The screen goes black. The music stops. It is dark and silent and then a confident, male voice comes on asking bluntly: *"Do you know where you're going when you die? We do."*

Then the sun comes up on the screen and the music becomes hopeful and inspiring and the voice says something about finding salvation and eternal life and then there is a picture of a local church—The Lighthouse Chapel on West Eighteenth Avenue—with its address, phone number, directions to the church, and worship times. I never went to that particular church to find out what happens when we die, but I know many in Eugene who did go—once, twice, maybe even three times a week. It was a very popular church.

Scholars have long theorized about the significance of death when it comes to religion: fear about death, making sense of death, hoping for life after death, and so on.

According to the anthropologist Bronislaw Malinowski (1954, 47), people are condemned to living their lives in the shadow of death,

"and he who clings to life and enjoys its fullness must dread the men-
ace of its end." For Malinowski, "of all sources of religion . . . death is
of the greatest importance." The psychologist Sigmund Freud (1961,
19) concurred, citing the "painful riddle of death" as a major source of
a sense of helplessness, which religion helps to alleviate.

Recent data indicate that belief in life after death is very strong
and widespread in our country:

- Roughly 80 percent of Americans believe in life after death.
- Two out of every three Americans expect to exist in some
  form following death, and most of them think their life after
  death will be a positive experience.
- 86 percent of Americans believe in Heaven; 71 percent believe in Hell.
- Over one-fourth of Americans surveyed believe in reincarnation.

The matter of death is clearly central when it comes to religion
(Gilman, 1923). But religion doesn't merely concern itself with what
happens when we die. Many would argue that matters of death are actually of much less importance than the lived religious experiences
that people have, such as personal and profound connections to God.
As Rodney Stark (1999) puts it, "normal people do talk to God"—and
such connections with the divine are undeniably important when it
comes to religion. And they are more common than you might think.

Consider my friend, Stewart Stein.[2]

I met Stewart in third grade. He was one of the brightest, friend-
liest, most charismatic, and most mature kids in the schoolyard. It
may seem odd to describe a third grader as "mature," but, well, that
was Stewart. We played on the same baseball team throughout elementary school. We had our bar mitzvahs during the same year in the
same synagogue. I accompanied him and his family on many a camp-
ing expedition in northern California throughout high school. We
lost touch during college.

And then one day while I was in graduate school I heard from a
friend of a friend that Stewart had become enlightened—that he was
a spiritual guru with followers and everything. It was a real shock. I
always assumed Stewart would become a corporate attorney or city

councilman or CEO of some corporation or agency—something respectable and "establishment." I was quite wrong. Stewart had turned out very differently. He was walking around barefoot, with long hair, beads around his neck, and leading his followers on spiritual retreats to northern Arizona. Fascinated, I called him up, and we began corresponding. I asked him about his new spiritual/religious identity. He explained to me that he had been living in Vermont for a while and had spent a year or two "in the personal growth community," by which he meant "workshops, seminars, [and] speaking engagements." And then he went on to describe explicitly two of his direct and personal encounters with God:

I spent the first twenty-five years of my life not believing in God, and then I started to open up to the idea of there being a God simply with the idea that it might make my life better. I certainly didn't buy the whole program hook, line and sinker. I just dipped my toes in the water to see how the water was. Imagine me at a spiritual healing school being totally triggered every time the teacher mentioned the word God! I was so opposed to it, but I was totally fascinated by the idea of energy, how it worked in our bodies and how it could be harnessed to create health and cure disease. . . . But God was a whole 'nother ballgame. It wasn't until I read a brochure from my second teacher that I ran into the house, threw everything down, and had a forty-five minute vent session where I literally called God every name in the book. Every swear word, every curse word, every rotten thing I'd ever felt towards God. Abandoned, shammed, tricked. You name it. It felt like five hundred years of anger and spite opened up and let loose. I ended up flat on my back, crying hysterically, finally ready to see if there was something there. And then this very gentle voice came to me and started telling me how much it loved me and how it never left me. Never.

And from a subsequent letter on another encounter with God:

So I'm sitting in the zen center . . . It's a Saturday, I think, and I'm facing the wall like everybody, when all of a sudden this really gentle energy appears in front of me. I sensed it just to my left near my shoulder. It wasn't a big deal. Just a presence.

And this voice inside of me says, "God?"
And this very gentle voice says, "Yes . . ."

It is so natural, so present, so not a big deal.
So I say, "Oh . . . nice to have you on board."
And the voice says, "Nice to have you on board."

Our correspondence broke off a couple of years ago. The last I heard, Stewart was living in northern California, leading very successful spiritual healing seminars. My old friend Stewart's personal experiences with God are certainly unique, but they aren't too far out of the ordinary. Truth is, most Americans claim to experience God in some deeply personal manner. Consider:

- 82 percent of Americans agree that they are "sometimes very conscious of the presence of God."
- 58 percent of Americans think about their relationship with God on a regular basis.
- One in three American teenagers claims to have personally experienced the presence of God.

As for myself, I haven't had any experiences like those of my friend Stewart—no direct, personal communication with God (or any deity, for that matter). To be perfectly honest, I can't even claim to have ever had what might be called a deeply religious, paranormal, mystical, life-changing spiritual experience. Sure, I've had wonderful, serene moments in my life, rare times when I felt a sense of wonder, awe, joy, serendipity, completeness, timelessness. These moments have a subtly ethereal, fleeting quality to them. They feel transcendent. Eating ripe wild blackberries while walking down a gravel road in the woods of Oregon by an old cemetery one August afternoon; surfing at Venice Beach; the night of the birth of my first daughter; the moment I saw my girlfriend (now wife) standing by the moonlit water's edge at Leo Carillo beach on a June night; listening to Nick Drake on rainy evenings; dancing to a great band at the Porter Quad on the UC Santa Cruz campus with painted, smiling faces all around me, sunshine splashing my body, and magic mushrooms turning me on; and so on. Such moments definitely evoke a powerful sense of the deep, mysterious goodness of existence and the tragic, fragile beauty of life. But I would hesitate to call these experiences deeply "religious" or "spiritual." And many would argue that without having had such an experience, I am missing a crucial element of religion. Indeed, according to some scholars, mystical experiences compose the very heart of religion.

In his book *The Idea of the Holy* (1952 [1917]), the theologian and philosopher Rudolph Otto argued that at the very core of religion was people's interaction with "the numinous"—a term which designates a feeling or experience of intense mystery, inexpressible majesty, a consciousness of the "wholly other," something beyond rational understanding, ineffable, a daunting, fascinating, terrifying, intoxicating sense of the *mysterium tremendum*. The psychologist and philosopher William James, in his classic *The Varieties of Religious Experience* (1936 [1902]), also emphasized mystical, spiritual, transcendent experiences as being at the root of religion. His appraisal of religion is replete with numerous accounts of people's personal, numinous experiences. Though less grandiose or dramatic than many of the accounts collected in James's book, here's one of my particular favorites:

> I have on a number of occasions felt that I had enjoyed a period of intimate communion with the divine. These meetings came unasked and unexpected, and seemed to consist merely in the temporary obliteration of the conventionalities which usually surround and cover my life . . . Once it was when from the summit of a high mountain I looked over a gashed and corrugated landscape extending to a long convex of ocean that ascended to the horizon, and again from the same point when I could see nothing beneath me but a boundless expanse of white cloud, on the blown surface of which a few high peaks, including the one I was on, seemed plunging about as if they were dragging their anchors. What I felt on these occasions was a temporary loss of my own identity, accompanied by an illumination which revealed to me a deeper significance than I had been wont to attach to life. It is in this that I find my justification for saying that I have enjoyed communication with God. Of course the absence of such a being as this would be chaos. I cannot conceive of life without its presence. (James 1936, 69).

I remember an anthropologist I met at a conference a couple of years ago telling me—over chips and beer—about her own life-changing spiritual experience. She too was on top of a mountain when she unexpectedly found herself enveloped in glowing white light, immersed in a feeling of love, safety, serenity—she knew it was the presence of God. Such experiences as the one I quoted from James's book or as described by the anthropologist I met at the conference are actually quite common. According to research undertaken by Andrew Greeley (1975), over a third of Americans answered "yes" to the following question: "Have you ever felt as though you were very close to a powerful, spiritual force that seemed to lift you out of yourself?" And more recent data from a Gallup survey conducted in 1996 soundly affirmed Greeley's data: 43 percent of American adults claim to have had an "unusual and inexplicable spiritual experience" and 36 percent of Americans surveyed answered "yes" to the question: "Have you ever had a religious experience—that is, a particularly powerful religious insight or awakening?" Of course, just what constitutes a religious experience is qualitatively different for every person. But the point is that religious experiences are not things that happen only to the prophets of old or to gurus who have been meditating for twenty years. Chances are, you yourself have had one—or know someone who has.

The mystery of death, communicating with God, experiencing the numinous—these are all important matters when it comes to religion. And, also important: prayer (Ladd and Spilka, 2002).

Earlier, I mentioned my mother-in-law. She is a born-again Southern Baptist Christian—and very big on prayer. She claims that prayer has dramatically changed her life for the better; from her relationship with her husband to her professional career, she swears by the power of prayer. She prays before every meal (out loud when we are at her house, silently when she is at ours). She prays whenever she can't sleep at night, or whenever she happens to feel the need throughout the day. One of my best friends from college, Jonah, who is an Orthodox Jew, also prays—at least three times a day. Another good friend of mine, Doug, who is in graduate film school with my wife and a recently converted Mormon (though not a "scriptural literalist," he is quick to point out), also prays a lot. Doug, Jonah, and my mother-in-law are not unusual. Regardless of what The Doors' front man Jim Morrison passionately shrieked about not being able to petition the Lord with prayer, note the following:

- 90 percent of Americans say they pray, a percentage which has held strong for over fifty years.

- Three in four adult Americans report praying on a daily basis.
- 58 percent of Americans claim to pray weekly.
- 97 percent of those who pray believe their prayers are heard, with 95 percent contending that their prayers have been answered.
- One quarter of those who pray report having heard a voice or seeing a vision as a result of their praying.

Personally, I'm pretty reluctant/skeptical/miffed when it comes to prayer. Sure, in moments of fear or anxiety I have sort of "deeply wished" that things would turn out all right. But I've never honestly believed that my deep wishing was being heard or considered by anyone or anything. Usually, my deep wishing just made me feel better at the moment—a quick mental/emotional balm in a time of great worry or stress. Anyway, I was discussing prayer with Doug the other night—respectfully expressing my skepticism of the whole business—and he challenged my criticisms, describing prayer as a very profound, crucial, and significant element in his life. I decided to ask him more about it. In a recent e-mail, I asked: *Why do you pray? What does prayer mean to you? What role does prayer play in your life? Can you give me specific examples of times when prayer was particularly meaningful or important in your life?*

Here are excerpts from his three page, single-spaced response:

Prayer is my entrance into faith. My faith began at a very specific moment, it was the first time I prayed. Throughout my life I had harbored substantial hostility towards religion. I was passionate about the idea that religion and spirituality couldn't even be considered legitimate fields of discourse . . . what still amazes me is that while believing these things I actually tried praying. One night before I was to teach a large climbing clinic at an indoor gym I just didn't feel ready at all. Without going into the ugly details of my life at that time, suffice it to say that severe depression, the ending of a long relationship, travel, and working too hard had worn me down . . . That night I prayed. My prayer began something like "I don't know if people who deny the existence of God can pray but . . ." My life didn't turn around right away, the climbing clinic I taught the next day wasn't the best ever, but I was profoundly changed as a person as a result of that prayer, and found myself praying the next day, and the next, and so on . . .

That first prayer was the first time I ever engaged faith and I think that's why it worked. Even though I was staunchly anti religious, what I actually did in the act of prayer was far more powerful than what I believed. This letting go of the rational is for me what makes prayer so delightful and freeing. As an intellectual I was driven by rational values of logic, reason, knowledge, etc. When I found myself deeply engaged in an act as irrational as trying to communicate with divinity through prayer I was stunned but, mostly, delighted by the paradox. Prayer can't be understood by means satisfying to the rational mind, nor should it be. It exists in a separate realm of human experience that does not bear the burden of explanation, proof, or even truth. I should say that when I refer to prayer as irrational I mean this in a completely positive sense, there is nothing pejorative in calling faith or prayer irrational. I celebrate the irrational nature of prayer for its being intuitive, inspirational, and emotional in nature. These three qualities describe both the means of communication with God and the means by which we enjoy the delights and rewards of prayer . . .

There are occasions when I pray for help creating a specific outcome but I can't bring myself to ask directly. I prefer to ask God to work on me to help me hone skills, to help me be attentive to the people around me, to support me in my efforts to gain greater spiritual insights, from these things favorable outcomes feel more likely to arise. Of course the problem of praying for a specific outcome is that prayers dissonant with God's will won't, by definition, be answered so I try not to guess what God's will is, rather I hope that he will support me in my attempts at spiritual growth and that I can apply such growth to practical situations when necessary.

Before moving to southern California my wife and I prayed a great deal about the move, we lacked resources, we worried about our safety, we knew that housing was expensive and hard to find, we had no idea of how the whole thing would work. The very first apartment we looked at was the one we took. It was cheap, in a great neighborhood, within walking distance of our church, had a great community of other people with young children living there. The way it worked out for us was amazing. Now is this proof of God's hand in our affairs? I can't say, after all that is a question that the rational mind asks and I don't care about that sort of thing. From a rational point of view it's possible that we just had wildly good luck. The fact of the matter is that in finding this apartment everything fell into place and all our fears were addressed. We felt very blessed and were so grateful to have found a new

home that addressed every issue that had arisen due to the move. Why ruin
such a wonderful experience trying to prove why it happened. In the end it
happened, we were blessed and we did indeed express our gratitude to God
through prayer . . .

Well said. (Thank you, Doug.)

Finally, some mention of congregating. There's a lot of it going on.
All around me, people are coming together for religious purposes,
joining religious organizations, meeting within congregational walls
to share religious experiences in a group setting. The Roman Catholic Church recently constructed an eleven-story, 57,000-interior-
square-foot congregational facility here in Los Angeles at a cost of
$200 million. Considering my immediate neighbors: Sandy to the
left of my house regularly attends Catholic mass, Jean and her family
to the right of my house regularly attend Christian Science services,
and Roy and his wife behind us are very active members of their liberal Lutheran church.

Ever since Émile Durkheim's classic within the sociology of religion, *The Elementary Forms of the Religious Life* (1915), scholars have
noted the importance of the social/communal when considering religion. The first American sociologist of religion, W. E. B. Du Bois,
was particularly struck by the social/communal aspects of religious
life, especially in his research among African Americans. Du Bois
emphasized the degree to which black churches were not merely
"spiritual" centers, but, even more so, "social" centers providing community, a sense of belonging, and a way to connect to others (Zuckerman 2000, 2002).

Church membership is quite widespread: almost 70 percent of
Americans are members of a church or synagogue; and 43 percent of
Americans attend religious services two or three times a month. Com-
munity—the communal element in religion—is definitely important.
Yes, religion involves faith and spiritual devotion, but as William Sims
Bainbridge (1997, 168) points out, it also involves "affiliation with a
social group." In fact, some people who lack faith, who don't believe in
God, and who don't have any inclination toward prayer—people who
could easily be labeled irreligious—still join congregations for the social and communal joys such membership affords (Kelley 1997).

My own parents belong to a religious congregation, a successful Reconstructionist synagogue in Pacific Palisades, California. And yet, like most Jews, my parents don't believe in God, don't consider the Bible holy, don't pray, and don't have "faith." They are essentially irreligious. And yet they belong to a religious congregation. I know that a major reason they belong is simply to be with other Jews. Attending a religious congregation is a very common way of maintaining a strong tie to people who share a similar history, heritage, and ethnic identity (see Herberg 1955). Stressing the social element of his congregational affiliation, my dad always used to say to me when I was young: "Sam goes to synagogue to talk to God. I go to synagogue to talk to Sam."

In writing this chapter, I asked my dad to explicitly discuss his reasons for belonging to a religious organization.

He replied (via e-mail):

I am most definitely a non-believer. I consider myself an atheist—not an agnostic—an atheist. I don't believe there is a "supreme being" or an afterlife, or in the efficacy of prayer—who is there to pray to? I believe that those who assert these things bear the burden of proof—and they have none sufficient to persuade me. I cannot remember at any time of my life, from my earliest childhood memories, ever believing in God and all that goes with it . . .

I, a non-believer, am a member of a religious organization because:

It's close by. I know the people who go there because they're from the community where I have lived for 36 years.

It makes me feel I'm part of something, a kind of Community . . .

It's "entertaining" to go there: the cantor, speakers, musical performances; afterward the oneg-shabbat *(oynig-shabes)[3] with food and socializing. The special attention the Cantor pays me. Seeing people I know there (Sam, not God). It lends a certain rhythm to life: Friday night,* shul.[4] *Mom seems to like it—so it's something we do together that is diverting . . . The rabbi does have a brain, and never says anything that makes me groan . . . all in all, I like him . . .*

My dad actually wrote a lot more (about his Jewish identity as a child growing up in the Bronx, about his move to Los Angeles and feelings of isolation, about wanting me and my brother to have a Jewish education, etc.), but I feel the above selection illustrates well enough the fact that people congregate for a variety of reasons, and not necessarily the typical reasons that come to mind when you think about people joining a "religious" organization.

So far, I have tried to convey just how much religion is all around me by discussing my friends, family, neighbors, national survey data, and so on. Throughout the discussion, I have briefly touched upon what I consider to be some of the more significant elements of religion: answers or explanations concerning the mystery of death, direct communication with God, religious or mystical experiences, prayer, and congregation. There are of course many more crucial aspects of religion: rituals, doctrine, faith, morality, scripture, music, education, proselytizing, sexual regulation, providing ultimate meaning, and the like. But this introduction was not meant to be comprehensive—I simply wanted to get the ball rolling by sharing a little bit about my world and the religion therein.

You may recall that at the end of the very first paragraph of this introduction, I quipped: "Some days it feels like the whole world is religious." That, of course, was a bit of an exaggeration. Somewhere between 8 and 15 percent of the U.S. population can be described as wholly nonreligious (Fuller 2001). According to statistics published in the *Los Angeles Times* (October 25, 2001, 23), approximately thirty million Americans claim to have "no religion." And personally, the truth is, while some of my best friends are indeed religious or spiritual, most aren't. Most of my closest friends are actually quite removed from religion, skeptical of its truth claims, suspicious of its practice, and dubious about its worth. My wife isn't religious. Neither is my brother. Nor are most of my cousins. And being a Jew who tends to socialize with other Jews, I am often in the company of the distinctly irreligious; Jews are perhaps the least religious "religious" group in the world.[5] Additionally, I am a social scientist—the least religious of the academic disciplines (Stark and Finke 2000)—and I'm a sociologist, no less. Most sociologists, at least from my personal experience, tend to be either irreligious or antireligious. So the fact is, I often dwell among the distinctly secular.

But unlike my wife and my closest friends and many of my fellow sociologists (Mills 1983; Ebaugh 2002), I am completely fascinated by religion. Utterly and hopelessly and unabashedly fascinated by it. I just can't get enough of it. Most of the irreligious people that I know don't really care much about religion. They either ignore it or are bored by it or assume it isn't all that significant or erroneously presume that it is dying out—or they just can't be bothered with it.

Not me. Religion is a personal fixation. I wonder how it is that millions of people can believe the manifestly implausible. I wonder how it is that millions of people can devote their lives to, and even die for, that which is ultimately irrational.[6] I wonder why some religions die out, while others enjoy tremendous success. I wonder why some religious entrepreneurs are labeled crazy by their surrounding society, while others enjoy widespread respect and support. I wonder why some people lose their faith, and why others suddenly attain theirs. I wonder why some countries are extremely religious (like Ireland), while others aren't at all (like Iceland). I am ceaselessly interested in the connection of religion to the arts, to politics, to sex, to war, to ethics, to race relations, to the media, to gender construction, to family life, to law—in short, I am ever drawn to pondering and studying the ways in which religion is affected by various aspects of society and, simultaneously, the ways in which various aspects of society are in turn affected by religion. Apprehending that dialectic is what the sociology of religion is all about.

Notes

1. All statistics/percentages cited in this chapter come from national survey data published by Gallup (1997), Gallup and Lindsay (1999), Greeley and Hout (1999), and Greeley (1995), unless otherwise noted.
2. Not his real name.
3. Hebrew (and Yiddish) for the weekly celebration with food and friends following services on Friday nights.
4. Yiddish for house of prayer/synagogue.
5. For instance, only 22 percent of American Jews claim that religion is "very important" in their lives (national average is 60 percent), and only 27 percent of American Jews claim to have attended church/synagogue within the seven days prior to being polled (national average is 60 percent). According to research by Andrew Greeley (1995), of all religious groups in America, Jews are the very least likely to attend church (synagogue), pray daily, believe in life after death, or believe that the Bible is the inspired word of God. Jewish religion is actually quite diluted in Israel as well, with almost half the Israeli population defining themselves

as "irreligious" (*lo dati*) and only approximately 20 percent defining themselves as Orthodox (Kedem 1995). It is actually more historically and sociologically accurate to consider Jews as constituting an ethnic group or people (*am*) that contains a religious component than constituting a "religion" per se (Kaplan 1981).

6. Leading sociologists of religion Stark and Finke (1993) take offense at the use of the word "irrational" when describing religion, automatically assuming that the word "irrational" is a pejorative put-down. It needn't be. Like Rudolph Otto (1952) and my friend Doug quoted earlier, I use the term "irrational" in a decidedly nonpejorative sense. Some of the most wonderful, noble, and sacred things in life are irrational, such as love, risk, art, sex, music, altruism, and so on.

1

SOCIOLOGY AND RELIGION

Every academic discipline, from philosophy to physics, has its particular "slant" on the subject of religion, its distinct perspective. This book is obviously about the *sociological* perspective on religion.

In order to explore the sociology of religion, I must begin with the first part—*sociology*—and then proceed to illustrate how it applies to the second part, religion. Of course, to briefly summarize sociology is no easy task. Every individual sociologist has his or her unique understanding of the discipline, and there will undoubtedly be those who find my attempt to describe sociology lacking. Nevertheless, here I go.

Sociologists, in the words of Peter Berger (1963, 18), are "intensively, endlessly, shamelessly" interested in humans. From the behavior of people in elevators to the racing of llamas, from beer drinking to breast implanting, from race relations to rug making—if it involves humans, sociologists are interested. Sociology is distinguished both by its subject matter (what sociologists actually study) and by its particular orientation/perspective (how sociologists look at the world).

Here then are my "top ten" components of sociology.

1. Sociologists study social groups.

Street gangs and student movements, baseball teams and Boy Scouts, lesbians and libertarians, marines and Mothers Against Drunk Driving, the Ku Klux Klan, the Black Panthers, animal rights activists, taxidermists—in short—any association of people you can think of, a sociologist has been, is, or will be studying it.

2. Sociologists study social interaction.

Have you ever been standing with a friend on a street corner, having a great conversation, when suddenly a third person joins you—notice how the dynamic suddenly changes? Have you ever noticed that your boyfriend or girlfriend acts differently when he or she is

17

with you alone than when his or her friends are around? These are just a couple of examples of the kinds of things "micro" sociologists study: how people interact with one another, how people present themselves to one another, how people's very identities change given various social contexts, circumstances, and forms of interaction (Simmel 1950; Goffman 1959; Garfinkel 1967).

3. Sociologists study social institutions and social structures.

Schools. The military. Corporations. Police departments. City hall. The government. Hospitals. Prisons. The family. Courts. Marriage. Industries. The media. Sports. The economy. Political systems. The workplace. The welfare system. And a whole lot more. Sociologists look at the ways certain social structures and institutions frame and shape our lives, greatly affecting where we live, how we live, who we live with—even how long we live.

4. Sociologists study social patterns.

Social patterns refer to everything from divorce rates to fashion trends, crime rates to how people kiss, rates of drug usage to what people eat. Personally, I like to ponder the social patterns (those primarily concerning race and gender) that can be observed at Los Angeles International Airport: the people who check bags on the curbside are almost always middle-aged black men. The flight attendants are almost always white women. The people working by the luggage x-ray machines are almost always young black women. The pilots are almost always white men. Why? Understanding and explaining such social patterns—how it is that certain jobs become gender and/or racially segregated, for instance—is a typical sociological concern.

5. Sociologists understand that an individual can be truly understood only within his or her sociohistorical context.

From reading assertions 1 to 4, one might get the impression that sociologists don't concern themselves with individuals. This is simply not so. Sociologists are very much concerned with individuals. But we do approach our study of the individual in a special, sociological way. To put it simply, we believe that the individual only "makes sense" when his or her social environment is taken into account. Though we are all individuals, we are individuals existing in specific points in history, in specific countries, in specific neighborhoods, in specific economies, in specific families. Where, when, and with whom we as individuals find ourselves living are all incredibly important factors in shaping our personal lives and identities. The way every individual dresses, the food she or he eats, the music she or he likes, his or her political opinions, the way she or he experiences love, the way she or he communicates, and so on, are all directly linked to specific sociohistorical circumstances beyond any one individual's control, or even consciousness.

As C. Wright Mills (1959, 7) taught, understanding the world sociologically involves perceiving the "intersections of biography and history within society." The point is that while we live our lives as individuals, experiencing personal circumstances, most aspects of our individual lives are actually quite enmeshed in historical processes and subject to specific social constraints. This leads us directly to the next important element of the sociological perspective.

6. Sociologists are interested in the ways in which individuals are shaped and influenced by their social environment.

In 1920, Amala and Kamala—two girls aged approximately nine—were discovered living underneath a giant anthill in an underground wolf den with a family of wolves, just outside the small town of Godamuri, India. It was speculated that they had been abandoned by their human parents at an early age and subsequently "adopted" by the wolves. Here are some of the characteristics of these two prepubescent girls as documented by those who found them. They moved about on all fours, like wolves. They didn't speak or respond to human language. They were unable to stand, walk, or run in an upright manner. They loved eating raw meat, especially carrion (they were observed aggressively chasing away large vultures from animal carcasses in order to get at the decaying flesh). They ate with their mouths only. They lapped water like dogs. They panted with their tongues out when it was hot. They growled and showed their teeth when frightened or threatened. They loved the night and the dark, but were skittish in the daylight. They howled at the moon. They weren't interested in other children, but preferred the company of dogs. In sum, they were agile, ferocious, and as wolflike as is humanly possible. Shortly after being discovered, they were brought to an orphanage, where Amala became sick and died. Kamala stayed at the orphanage, however, and over the course of several years eventually learned how to stand and walk upright, eat and drink with her hands, and feel comfortable in the daylight. She was also able to learn some words—about forty-five in all. Kamala became sick and died in 1929, around the age of seventeen.

The implications of this story of Amala and Kamala are staggering (Candland 1993; Gesell 1940). This little-known but very well documented case comes closest of all such similar cases to "proving" that our identities are largely determined by our social environment. Can you imagine what a different person you would be had you lived most of your childhood in a wolf den? Would you have the same taste in music—would you even "understand" music? Would you have the same sense of humor? The same love life? What about you would be the same, if anything?

We may all be born with certain innate characteristics, skills, tendencies, and traits, but these are mere potentialities—potentialities that can only be "brought to life" given external (social) stimuli. And the whole point is that different social environments will suppress or awaken different innate potentialities. As Michael Schwalbe (2001, 19) succinctly asserts, "if you had been born into a different social world you would be a different person."

7. Sociologists are fascinated by nonconformity and the ways in which people resist or change the social forces that surround them.

In my high school, it was a norm that girls shaved their legs. Any girl who didn't shave her legs was considered "gross" and faced ridicule and ostracism. This norm was what Émile Durkheim (1982 [1895]) would call a "social fact." Social facts are subtle but ever-pervasive rules, norms, and values that most of us succumb to and "obey." They shape and mold us throughout our lives, often without our even being aware of it. As I said, the girls in my high school shaved their legs. And they didn't necessarily feel forced to do so; they honestly liked having shaved legs and sincerely felt that not having shaved legs would be unattractive and weird. But there was one girl in my high school who resisted this social fact: Melody Weeks. She refused to shave her legs. And she was ridiculed and ostracized by many as a result. Though it may have been hard to be teased or shunned, Melody clearly had a firm sense of herself and a certain spirit of inner strength that I always admired and envied.

Sociologists are fascinated by deviance: the violation of social norms, the resisting of societal pressures. Deviance can be heinous (molesting children) or heroic (saving the lives of children being hunted by Nazis). But whenever people go against the grain, resist the rules of society, violate accepted laws, don't do what others expect them to do, we are dealing with an aspect of human behavior of major sociological concern (Becker 1963; Goode 2002). Deviant behavior illustrates the fact that people aren't completely obedient. Most of us most of the time may behave like sheep—happily conforming to society's rules and expectations—but not all of us, and not always. While we are all inevitably shaped by our society, it is never completely a one-way street; sometimes some of us "act back" and become the determining creators of our social world. Instances of deviance illustrate the reality that there is always a degree of human freedom, of individualism, of human agency at play in the world. Sociologists revel in the fact that there will always be a Melody Weeks, a Rosa Parks, or a Margaret Sanger out there to stir things up, resist, and maybe even change the very social framework itself.

8. Sociologists are fascinated by "the social construction of reality."

In the words of Kanagy and Kraybill (1999, 20), "We people are the architects of our social world, but one of the remarkable aspects of social life is how easily we forget who built it." Sociologists go out of their way never to forget. We are always cognizant of the degree to which much of our world is humanly created, in obvious and not so obvious ways. Think about it: The ring you will give your partner upon marriage is obviously made by humans, but so is the very institution of marriage. The birth certificate which records your race was obviously made by humans, but so is the very concept of "race" to begin with. The lipstick you or your girlfriend wears is obviously made by humans, but so is your very concept of "beauty." The passport which proves your citizenship of a given country was obviously made by humans, but so are countries.

Many things that we take for granted as being "real" (i.e., permanent or natural), such as countries, money, what constitutes a family, what love is, how time operates, what constitutes a crime, are largely the result of human culture. As Kanagy and Kraybill (1999, 18) put it, "human values, ideas, and patterns of behavior did not drop miraculously from heaven but were fashioned by humans over many centuries."

9. Sociologists debunk.

Once you start looking at the ways in which so many taken-for-granted aspects of our world are socially constructed, once you start carefully observing the pervasiveness of specific social patterns and the grand influence of social institutions on individual lives, an inevitable consequence is what Peter Berger called an "unmasking tendency" that is inherent in the sociological enterprise. For Berger (1963, 23), "the first wisdom of sociology is this—things are not what they seem."

What the government says, what the media declare, what corporate executives claim, what professors profess, may not always be true. Sociologists don't draw conclusions about the world based on common sense, for the things that "everybody knows as true" often aren't (Ruane and Cerulo 2000). For example, throughout the 1990s, most Americans believed that crime in America was getting worse and worse. But just the opposite was actually happening; rates of murder and all other violent crimes were at thirty-year lows (Glassner 1999; Kappeler, Blumberg, and Potter 2000). How do we know? Evidence. Data. Research. Studies. Martin Marger (2002, 7) clearly explains that sociological conclusions are based on "empirical substantiation," that is, claims made by sociologists are "subject to inspection and investigation . . . founded on data collected through research, which can be verified by others." Because sociologists base their conclusions on careful research—which often reveals the nebulous, contradictory, ambiguous, and multifaceted nature of social realities—they are always skeptical of simplistic answers to complex problems. Again from Kanagy and Kraybill (1999, 104): "Sociologists choose to reflect before judging, to challenge before agreeing."

10. Sociology entails a critical approach to understanding the world.

One of the founders of sociology was the radical social critic Karl Marx. His favorite motto was *De omnibus dubitandum*—"one ought to question everything." Along with the debunking tendency within sociology discussed above is an explicitly critical disposition. What do we mean by "critical"? Evan Willis (1996, 83) explains:

> [T]he term *critical* does not mean being negative. Rather, the term is used . . . in the sense of being reflexive or skeptical about the social world . . . engaging in systematic doubt about accounts of the social world . . . [I]n exercising a critical sensibility, sociologists try to uncover and expose the ambiguities, misrepresentations, distortions, and even falsehoods in competing explanations for particular social phenomena.

No matter what we study, be it educational systems or country clubs, sociologists sniff out racism, sexism, classism, homophobia, hypocrisy, inequality, corruption, and social injustice as best we can. It is not that sociologists have nothing better to do than find flaws in society. Rather, sociology is simply the discipline most actively engaged in questioning, doubting, and critiquing what Peter Berger (1963, 35) dubbed "the official versions of reality." And ultimately this critical disposition of sociology is embedded in a desire to improve the world, to ponder alternatives toward enhancing human freedom (Scimecca 1995). As Evan Willis (1996) notes, there are several key questions the sociologist is always asking, no matter what subject he or she may be investigating: What's happening? Why? What are the consequences? How do we know? (and perhaps most important) *How could it be otherwise?*

Well, there you have it: my explanation of what sociology is all about. Now I'll discuss how the above aspects of sociology relate specifically to religion.

1. Sociologists study social groups.

Religions are, if nothing else, social groups. Whether it be college students who meet in their dorm rooms once a week for Bible study or established congregations, a handful of pagans who gather in the woods at summer solstice or million-member denominations, religious bodies are quite obviously social collectives. When one is studying the dynamics of group affiliation and the formation of social confederacy, religious groups clearly provide excellent samples.

2. Sociologists study social interaction.

Religion may entail interaction with the divine, but it also entails interaction among humans. Circumcisions, pilgrimages, christenings, bar mitzvahs, confessions, peyote ceremonies, church picnics—religion is dripping with social interaction. Ever since Émile Durkheim's classic treatise *The Elementary Forms of the Religious Life* (1915)—in which Durkheim posited that social interaction was actually the source, the very *cause* of religion—sociologists have paid careful attention to the rich and dramatic varieties of social interaction that compose religious phenomena.

3. Sociologists study social institutions and social structures.

Religion—by definition—is a social institution. And in many parts of the world, religion is one of the most powerful, all-pervasive social institutions out there. It thus makes sense that many of the founding sociologists such as Émile Durkheim, Max Weber, George Simmel, W. E. B. Du Bois, Charlotte Perkins Gilman, and Friedrich Engels wrote and theorized extensively about religion. Sociologists of religion are interested not only in analyzing religion as a social institution in its own right, but also in understanding how religion influences, and is influenced by, other major social institutions. For instance, the single most famous and widely recognized seminal study within the sociological canon is Max Weber's *The Protestant Ethic and the Spirit of Capitalism* (2002 [1904]). In this classic study, Weber explores the ways in which specific Protestant/Calvinist religious beliefs played a decisive role in the development of modern western capitalism.

4. Sociologists study social patterns.

Do women attend religious services more often than men? Are blacks more likely to believe in the existence of Satan than whites? Do Jews tend to vote more liberal than Christians? Do religious people divorce less frequently than the nonreligious? Sociologists of religion have their work cut out for them in exploring the plethora of patterns that emerge concerning religion in society. The most hotly debated topic within the sociology of religion during the past decade has revolved around a basic question of one particular social pattern: whether or not people are more or less religious today than they were in the past—the matter of secularization (Swatos and Olson 2000; Bruce 1992).

5. Sociologists understand that an individual can be truly understood only within his or her sociohistorical context.

To put it simply, an individual can be a member of a particular religion only if that religion exists when he or she does. Furthermore, geography (where a person exists) is key (Park 1994). An individual born in Sri Lanka is much more likely to be Buddhist than an individual born in Honduras, who will most likely be Catholic (O'Brien and Palmer 1993). My friend Kent describes himself as "nothing" in terms of a religious identity. But he isn't "nothing" in a sociohistorical vacuum. His parents were also "nothing"; they didn't raise Kent with any particular religious education or involvement. Furthermore, Kent grew up in a largely secular enclave and attended school in west Los Angeles with few overtly religious kids or teachers. Additionally, Kent lives in a time in history and within a culture in which religion isn't imperative, lack of religion isn't illegal or suspect, and being "nothing" is considered quite normal. In short, an individual's personal religious identity (or lack thereof) is greatly influenced by where, when, and among whom that individual lives.

6. Sociologists are interested in the ways in which individuals are shaped and influenced by their social environment.

Of the many components of the social environment that are important in shaping and influencing how individuals live their lives, religion is certainly crucial. Religious values, religious norms—in short, religious culture—greatly affect how people understand themselves and others. Sociologists are fascinated by the affects of religion on people's sex lives, political views, national identities, economic activities, eating habits, career choices, marital relations, and, conversely, how such things affect people's religious identities.

7. Sociologists are fascinated by deviance, nonconformity, and the ways in which people resist or change the social forces that surround them.

The most dramatic role that deviance plays in the realm of religion is the development of new religious traditions. After all, every new religious movement ever established was created through deviance;

some individual or group of individuals decided to go against the norm, to rebel against the established order, to defy the authorities, and even the law. Paul, Muhammad, Siddhartha, Guru Nanak, Vardhamana Mahavira, Baha'Allah, Martin Luther, Joseph Smith—all were religious deviants who, rather than passively accept and internalize the religious life around them, broke free and successfully acted against the prevailing religious system to create something new.

8. Sociologists are fascinated by "the social construction of reality."

It is simply unavoidable: the sociological perspective opens up the possibility that religion may very well be a social construction. When one is viewing the world sociologically, it is nearly impossible to keep from asking: Is religion truly something received from Above, or is it actually something developed down here by human beings? Countless social theorists throughout the past two centuries have suspected that religion may not necessarily be an outgrowth, reaction, or response to the divine/supernatural. They have argued that religion is more likely an outgrowth of human culture—a product of human psychological, sociological, and even neurological or physiological processes (Thrower 1999; Turner 1983; Hinde 1999; Guthrie 1993; Shermer 2000). As Peter Berger (1967, 180) admits, "sociological theory must, by its own logic, view religion as a human projection."

A rarely cited but brilliant essay titled "Sociological Theory and Religious Truth," by Benton Johnson (1977), thoroughly discusses the fact that considering the possibility that religion may be a social construction is simply unacceptable to the deeply religious. Indeed, it is generally understood as an outright *hostile* proposition. After all, suggesting that religion is a social construction threatens to destroy the very cosmos of the deeply religious. And so this is where things start to get sticky. This is where the sociological view of religion and the religious view of religion begin to come into clearest conflict.

According to Randall Collins (1992, 30), "There are two obvious positions that you can take about religion. Either you believe it or you don't: in one case it is a supreme Reality that transcends everything sociology is concerned with; in the other it is an irrational superstition about things that don't exist." Most sociologists tend to be skeptical of religion—as are most social scientists in general

(Wuthnow 1989; Thalheimer 1973). And most sociologists do tend to view religion as socially constructed at best or "irrational superstition" at worst. However, there *are* religious sociologists (Fraser and Campolo 1992), as well as religious sociologists of religion (see Stark and Finke 2000). Even Peter Berger, one of the leading sociologists of religion, is a man of faith, at least as expressed in his book *A Rumor of Angels* (1970). In that book, Berger argues that despite all of sociology's penetrating insights, a case can still be made for religious faith and a belief in divinely generated "transcendental truths." Berger further explores his personal Christian faith in relation to sociology in *The Heretical Imperative* (1979) and *The Precarious Vision* (1961).

Certainly many sociologists fall somewhere between convinced atheist and faithful believer. That's why I find Collins's mutually exclusive dichotomy quoted above as too extreme. Rather than an either/or situation (religion is *either* completely God-given *or* completely socially constructed), it is possible to conceive of a perspective that encompasses a continuum. On the one polar extreme, everything about religion is of divine origin. On the opposite polar extreme, everything about religion is of human origin. On this continuum, however, there is room for middle ground, room to meander. For example, one can believe that the "heart" or "root" of a given religion is of divine origin, while various trappings, layers, or components are socially constructed. One can believe that the underlying "impulse" of religion (to connect with the transcendent) is mystical, eternal, and otherworldly in nature, but that what becomes of this impulse (how it is directed, channeled, understood) is largely a societal/cultural phenomenon. In other words, one can accept both: certain aspects of religion may be of human origin, while others may not. Of course, determining which is which is what we all get to happily argue about to no end!

As can be expected, the "devout" in each camp will find a middle-ground approach unacceptable. The "extreme" sociologist will argue that religion is completely socially constructed and there is simply no empirical evidence for accepting divine intervention or existence (an essentially atheistic approach). And the "extreme" religious believer will argue that his or her religion is completely of divine origin, with very little or nothing about it being the result of social construction (an essentially fundamentalist approach). What is interesting, however, is that the extreme sociologist (atheist) and the devoutly religious (fundamentalist) are actually not so far apart from one another in their understanding of religion as one might think. They may appear to be on opposite sides of a wide intellectual chasm—but it isn't so. After all, the extreme sociologist sees 100 percent of all religions as social constructions, while the religious fundamentalist sees 99 percent of religions as social constructions—*all religions except his or hers!* That is, most deeply religious people can entertain the notion that *all other religions* are of human origin, just not their own.

9. Sociologists debunk.

Debunking within the sociology of religion expresses itself in two basic directions: (1) debunking "commonsense" views of and ideas about religion held throughout the wider society, and (2) debunking various religious truth claims themselves.

The first—debunking commonsense views of and ideas about religion held throughout society—involves using the tools of sociological research to dispel taken-for-granted truths about religion that aren't actually true. For example, consider the widely held view that certain religious groups "brainwash" their adherents. This is such a commonly held belief that most people are shocked when I tell them that brainwashing is actually an unfounded myth. Decades of sociological research have convincingly shown that brainwashing simply does not occur (Richardson and Introvigne 2001; Richardson 1993a; Dick 1990; Barker 1984; Bromley and Richardson 1983; Bainbridge 1978). Most people who check out "cults" don't join them, people who do join often leave of their own volition, and people who claim they were brainwashed tend to be ex-believers who need a way to justify/rationalize behavior and beliefs they no longer approve of or subscribe to (Wessinger 2000). But more important, there is simply no valid, empirical proof of "mind control" or the ability of members of small religious groups to somehow alter the brain functioning of members to do or think things they otherwise would not.

The second aspect of sociological debunking involves critically examining religious truth claims themselves. This may be as mundane as challenging church attendance statistics, revealing that not as many people are actually active members of congregations as the clergy may claim. For example, Catholic figures of church membership "flatter to deceive" in that they count everyone who has ever been baptized as a member, whether or not they have any subsequent religious involvement (Bruce 1999a). Or sociological debunking may be as dramatic as revealing that the outlined image of the Virgin Mary appearing on the windows of a city building in Clearwater, Florida, in 1996—which attracted throngs of faithful worshippers—was actually nothing more than a coincidentally formed image caused by a film of oil from a nearby palm tree sprayed onto the windows by sprinklers (Shermer 2000).

Sociologists simply do not take religious truth claims for granted as the final word on reality. What is absolute truth as divinely revealed to the firm religious devotee "ain't necessarily so" to the sociological investigator. Take one of the fastest-growing religions in the world today: the Church of Jesus Christ of Latter-day Saints, commonly known as Mormons (Stark 1996b). The Book of Mormon—the central component of Mormon scripture—claims that Native Americans are the descendants of Middle Eastern Jews who sailed from ancient Israel to North America (traveling some sixteen thousand miles by boat) approximately twenty-six hundred years ago. For the social scientist, however, this just "ain't necessarily so." In fact, it is outright implausible. There is no convincing evidence of this historical claim, and there is not a single non-Mormon archaeologist, anthropologist, or historian who gives any credence to this religious theory of history and transcontinental migration (Persuitte 2000). Even recent genetic/DNA analysis proves that the theory of Native Americans being the descendants of ancient Israelites is blatantly false (Lobdell and Stammer 2002).

To be sure, the job of the sociologist is not to argue these matters with faithful believers. The sociologist studying Mormonism is not out there to deconvert people, engage in historical or theological debates, destroy worldviews, or the like. Rather, we are curious intellectual investigators, intensely seeking to understand how it is that people can believe that which lacks reasonable evidence. We are fascinated by, and seek to explore as soberly as possible, how people can believe the unbelievable. We do not engage in such work to be disrespectful or pugnacious, but because we yearn to comprehend.

Again—and this point must be stressed, as I am sure many will react to this discussion defensively—we do not study Mormonism or Scientology or Judaism or Sikhism or Wicca to prove such religions "wrong" and subsequently deconvert their adherents. We study these religious systems because they intrigue us and we yearn to understand how it is that our fellow human beings can join groups and claim ideological devotion to belief systems which, to the outside observer, appear unusual, counterintuitive, or in outright contradiction to what we know of reality.

Of course, it often boils down to this thing called "faith." The religious believer has it (at least concerning his or her particular religion), and the sociologist doesn't. As Meredith McGuire (1997, 7) explains:

> The religious perspective on human life often produces a very different picture of that reality than does a sociological perspective. What is relevant to the religious believer may be irrelevant or inadmissible evidence to the sociologist . . .
>
> The sociological perspective, by definition, lacks a key religious quality—faith. The believer accepts certain beliefs and meanings on faith. Faith implies taking certain meanings or practices for granted, implicitly trusting, not questioning. By contrast, the sociologist does not take the believer's meanings for granted but takes them as an object of study.

There are certainly sociologists of religion who would argue that debunking the truth claims of a given religion is not part of our job at all. They would stress that such activity is beyond the scope of our discipline. For example, the founding sociologist of religion Max Weber declared that "from an evaluative standpoint" the Book of Mormon "would have to be called a 'hoax'"—but he then quickly added that "sociology is not concerned with such questions" (quoted in Gerth and Mills 1946, 246). As the contemporary sociologist of religion Steve Bruce (1996, 38) has remarked, "whether any particular religion is true is a theological, not a sociological, question."

So long as religions limit their assertions to matters pertaining to God and Heaven and the spiritual/otherworldly, then Bruce is correct: the sociologist has nothing to say on such matters. But religions don't do that. Religions make claims not only about God and Heaven and the spiritual realm, but also about people, history, government, society, and the here and now. Often these claims are posited as factual. The fact is, religions *never* limit their rhetoric to the otherworldly. They always pronounce upon *this* world, *this* earth, *this* reality. And when they do so, we have every right (indeed, the responsibility) to investigate and challenge their assertions. Let me put it this way: If a religion simply claims that "God is Love," then, as Bruce argues, questioning or analyzing such an assertion is theology, not sociology. But if a religion claims that "God is Love . . . *and he was here last night in our house wearing a white robe and he gave us this book which details who people may or may not have sex with*," the sociologist has plenty to investigate and pronounce upon: Did a man actually show up at their house dressed in a white robe? Was he really from another plane of existence? How do we know? Where did the book really come from? How do we know? In short, any claim asserted as factual concerning what occurs in *this* world and *this* reality—be it asserted by a steelworkers' union, a corporate think tank, a communist party pamphlet, a soccer mom, a senator, a member of the Lesbian and Gay Alliance, a cadre of sociologists, *or a religious group*—is fair game for sociological inquiry and (as the case may be) sociological debunking.

And yet, many scholars just don't think so. They urge that we social scientists give religious groups some sort of immunity from our investigations. According to the sociologist of religion Betty Scharf (1970), when it comes to the actual validity of religious beliefs, sociologists must remain "silent." The respected social anthropologist Clifford Geertz (1973, 123) has argued that when studying religious groups

> There remains the hardly unimportant questions of whether this or that religious assertion is true . . . *But such questions cannot even be asked, much less answered*, within the self-imposed limitations of the scientific perspective. [emphasis added]

Bryan Wilson (1982) concurs, arguing that the sociologist mustn't be concerned with the "truth" of religious beliefs. Andrew Greeley (1982, 5) joins the resounding chorus, declaring that determining whether a religious account of reality is true or not "is a matter which goes beyond social science." Chalfant, Beckley, and Palmer (1994, 19) agree.

I respectfully but vehemently disagree with the above scholars and any social scientist who would give religious truth claims a "free pass." Assertions of truth made by religious groups should always be questioned and investigated, as should assertions of truth posited by any group we care to study. If I am studying a group of Christian Scientists who claim that their prayers can cure cancer, it is incumbent upon me as a sociological investigator to see if these claims are actually true. If I am not convinced that their prayers have demonstrable healing powers—*but they think they do*—then this is certainly a major part of the story and of paramount sociological concern. If I am studying a group of Rastafarians who claim that their recently deceased spiritual leader was the modern-day embodiment of a reincarnated Jesus Christ, and I find proof of such a claim lacking—*but they are firmly convinced*—again, I am faced with a crucial element of their religion which demands exploration and explanation. Unless the sociologist is an unquestioning, faithful devotee of the given religious group he or she is studying, the very ethos of sociological investigation will tend toward debunking. It is simply the nature of the beast.

And again, let's keep in mind that the deeply religious are happy with and quite supportive of sociological, investigative, debunking inquiries—as long as they are directed at *other* religions and not their own.

My own sensibilities on this matter of sociological debunking and religious truth have been well expressed by Michael Shermer (2000, x):

> When people say they believe in God because it comforts them, because they have faith, because of personal revelation . . . I have no qualms . . . But when others say they can *prove* God, *prove* that their religion is the right one . . . such claims demand a scientific and rational analysis.

10. Sociology entails a critical approach to understanding the world.

In connection with what has been discussed above, we, as sociologists, always take a questioning, skeptical view of all social phenomena—and that applies to our study of religion as well. In other words, for sociologists of religion, nothing is sacred, even when studying a realm of humanity based on the sacred. We do not shy away from probing matters of sexism, racism, homophobia, exploitation, corruption, and so on. Our goal at the outset may not necessarily be to expose or sensationalize these things in our studies, but if we do find them, we certainly would not sweep them under the rug. Christel Manning's (1999) thoughtful study of women and religion, *God Gave Us the Right*, is an excellent example of employing a critical approach to the study of religion. Manning sought to understand women who join conservative or fundamentalist religious traditions. She relied upon an empathetic methodology wherein she tried to really get to know and be open to the women she studied. However, along with her openness and empathy toward her subjects, she still managed to critically analyze and expose various contradictions and inconsistencies, specifically in relation to patriarchal gender norms. As Manning (1999, 150) discusses:

> [The women] claim to reject feminism, yet they clearly embrace some feminist values. They want women to have equality and authority in work and in politics, but they are willing to give up on those things in church and synagogue. Evangelical women say a wife must submit to her husband, but almost none of them do.

Manning's study wasn't about debunking religion or exposing the inconsistencies or hypocrisy of her subjects. But because of her sociological approach, how women struggle with gender issues, sometimes successfully, sometimes not, was fair game for intellectual inquiry.

The critical sociological stance when studying religion can be problematic, and inevitably betrays the fact that we are fundamentally outsiders to the very phenomenon we seek to understand and explain.

Can you imagine trying to study, understand, and explain Beatles fans and decades of Beatlemania, while not being able to actually hear the Beatles' music for yourself? Could a deaf person ever really "get" (understand and explain) what this love of the Beatles is all about? The same question could be leveled at the nonreligious sociologist of religion: How can you really understand religion if you are "deaf" to its "music"? Some top scholars of religion have gone so far as to declare that nonreligious people simply cannot study religion at all; Stark and Finke (2000, 15) have argued that only "persons of faith" are capable of being "truly scientific" when it comes to studying religion.

Ultimately, this matter is one that confronts nearly all social scientific research, not merely that which deals with religion. Being an outsider to the very phenomena we wish to study is what social science is often all about—whether we are studying domestic workers, football players, or religious groups. As outsiders, we simply cannot get at all of The Truth. But we can still offer significant and important insights. One need not be a person of color or a committed racist to generate significant insights about racism in society. One need not be a radical environmentalist or a corporate polluter to generate significant insights about environmental issues. One need not be a member of the capitalist aristocracy or a factory worker in Indonesia in order to generate significant insights about the nature of global capitalism. Though Stark and Finke (2000)—as quoted above—believe that only the religious are truly capable of studying religion, I passionately disagree. Parents are not the only people capable of studying parenting. Doctors are not the only people capable of studying the medical industry. Fascists are not the only people capable of studying fascism. Artists are not the only people capable of studying art. Prostitutes are not the only people capable of study prostitution. Beatles fans are not the only people capable of studying the Beatles. And so it goes for religion (McCutcheon 1999, 2001).

Yes, being an outsider to religion means that there are just some crucial matters that we will simply never understand. But this rule also applies to the insider: the religious are also hindered in understanding some very important matters that can only be grasped from the outside. Neither the sociological (outsider) perspective nor the religious (insider) perspective on religion has a monopoly on truth. Both have their own particular insights. Both are important and essential.

As Bryan Wilson (1982, 14) has said:

> We may, of course, concede the obvious fact that, at one level, the sociologist will never understand as much as does a believer . . . At another level, however, since he sees from the outside, he may acquire a much sharper perspective about a religion . . . than is possible for those who are committed and who can only see from the inside.

2

TIME AND PLACE

Both sociology and psychology are interested in understanding and explaining humans. But they go about these tasks quite differently. Psychologists generally focus upon phenomena and processes that exist or occur beneath the skin: the mind, personality, brain functioning, cognitive processes, neurological activity, chemical reactions. In contrast, sociologists generally focus upon phenomena and processes that occur and exist outside the skin: social patterns, cultural norms, institutional forces, media influence, and so on. This difference of focus plays itself out quite prominently in the psychological versus sociological study of religion. As Malcolm Hamilton (1995, 21) puts it, "Psychological theories hold that religion is an affair of the individual and springs from sources within the individual, whereas sociological theories hold that religion is an affair of the group or society and that individual religiosity stems from social sources."

Psychologists of religion tend to explain religiosity by looking "inside" humans, hoping to find explanations of religious belief/activity in humans' psychophysiological makeup (Byrnes 1984). For instance, Michael Persinger (1987) has written a book titled *Neuropsychological Bases of God Beliefs* in which he offers an analysis of the role of temporal lobes, hormonal processes, and brain components (such as the hippocampus and amygdala) in explaining religiosity. Michael Shermer (2000, 47) speaks of a "Belief Engine" that is simply "part of our nature, built into our neuronal mainframe." Stressing neural circuitry and electrical brain activity as being central to religiosity is actually quite popular these days. In May of 2001, *Newsweek* ran the following cover story: "God and the Brain: How We're Wired for Spirituality."

While this research is important and interesting, it has its limits. Neuropsychological approaches to religion can certainly get us thinking about the ways in which humans are pattern-seeking animals, or how brain waves may alter significantly during prolonged meditative trances, but they can't tell us much about specific religious beliefs or actual religious identity. That's where I believe the importance of social interaction comes in, especially the role and impact of family, friends, neighbors, nation, and various sociocultural and historical processes. After all, exploring temporal lobe activity, genetic predispositions, hormonal differentiation, or synapses can't explain why some people are Quakers and others Sufi, or why some people believe that God had a son through a virgin woman and subsequently allowed that son to be painfully executed in order to save humans from everlasting torment in hell. Brain chemistry simply doesn't explain why some people are agnostic and others aren't. For instance, over the past one hundred years, the people of England and the Netherlands have become significantly less religious in terms of both belief and church attendance. Why? I doubt that this dramatic drop in religiosity is a result of changes in their temporal lobes or a lack of oil in their "Belief Engines." The changes are better explained by taking into account a variety of economic, political, historical, national, and social developments (Bruce 2001; Grotenhuis and Scheepers 2001; Verweij, Ester, and Natua 1997).

So what then does make one person a Hindu and another person a Sikh? Why are some parts of the world largely Buddhist and other parts Muslim? Why do some people believe in reincarnation, while others believe in Heaven and Hell? Why do some countries have extremely high rates of religiosity, while others extremely low? The answer—I would posit again—lies not within our internal biological chemistry or brain functioning or personalities or rational calculations, but stems from our interaction in a specific sociocultural environment and our biographical intersection with history in society. As Batson, Schoenrade, and Ventis (1993, 50) explain, "In spite of the popular view that our religion, or lack of it, is a freely chosen and very personal matter, much social-psychological theory and research points to a very different answer: Our religious beliefs and experiences are determined by our social environment."

In truth, *where we were born* and *who we live among* have an unparalleled determining influence on our religious identity (Bruce 1999a, 126–127). In the previous chapter, on page 25, I stated the following:

"an individual can be a member of a particular religion only if that religion exists when he or she does. Furthermore, geography (where a person exists) is key (Park 1994). An individual born in Sri Lanka is much more likely to be Buddhist than an individual born in Honduras, who will most likely be Catholic."

I'd like to develop this thought in greater detail. In this chapter I'd like to focus on the above statement's underlying theoretical thrust, namely: *religious identity is largely determined by, and always dependent upon, factors of time and place.* The sociology of religion begins with the understanding that where a person (or group) lives—and when—greatly affects his or her (or its) religious identity (Kelley and De Graaf 1997). The likelihood that a child born this morning in Sakakah, Saudi Arabia, will be Mulsim is far, far, far greater than the likelihood that she or he will be Episcopalian or a worshipper of the Aztec mother-goddess Tonantzin. The truth is, the overwhelming majority of people who are Muslim or some other religion today aren't Muslim or some other religion because of brain chemistry or even some individual/personal choice or life event. While there are always the notable exceptions, most people who are Muslim or some other religion today are not such because of genetics or even personal preference. Rather, they were born at a specific time in human history and in a particular place (i.e., city, state, or region) that made such a religious identity possible or, rather, inevitable—if not downright imperative.

Of course, certain religions do grow and expand, including Islam in particular, which obviously means that pockets of humanity—various individuals and groups—do change their religious affiliation now and then. So personal choice and individual preference are undeniable factors. But even such conversions follow the same confining limitations of time and place: a man or woman or town or community or tribe can only be converted to a new religion which focuses its missionary activity in a certain place and at a certain time.

Let me give an elaborate example/illustration.

Between 80 and 90 percent of Costa Ricans are Catholic. Why? After all, they could just as easily be nearly all Buddhist or Jewish or worshippers of Odin. So why Catholic? Do they have certain Catholic brain structures? Of course not. Do they all just "like" or "prefer"

Catholicism better than all the other religious options out there—that is, do most people in Costa Rica periodically compare and contrast the costs and benefits of all existing religions and then consistently and nearly unanimously agree that Catholicism is simply the best choice? There are too many obvious problems with such an egregiously simplistic, insufficiently sociological "rational choice" explanation.[1]

Well, OK, so how about if we ask some Costa Ricans why they are Catholic? What if I just randomly picked a name out of a Costa Rican phone book and called the number and asked the person on the other end why she or he is Catholic? My experience tells me that the person would probably stress matters of personal or theological preference, such as:

- It is the best religion
- It is the one true religion of God
- She or he knows that Jesus died for her or him
- She or he enjoys the blessings of the Virgin Mother, and so on.

The individual might even go so far as to mention that she or he is a Catholic because "that's what my parents were," or "that's how I was raised," or simply because "that's what we Costa Ricans are." But these responses merely bolster exactly what it is I am trying to figure out: why Costa Ricans are Catholic.

This whole matter became of interest to me when I was on a two-week vacation in Costa Rica a few years ago with my girlfriend (now wife), Stacy. At the end of our trip we arrived on the serene and luscious Nicoya Peninsula, where we found beautiful, empty beaches swelling with green-blue, gentle waves and verdant jungles laced with garrulous monkeys and more litchis than a tropical fruit lover such as myself could ever dream of. Our small hotel was in the tiny village of Playa Samara, but one day we ventured out to the central hub of the region, the small town of Nicoya. Nicoya is a calm, humble town with dirt roads and small houses and lots of kids playing and plenty of old men and women sitting on their porches whiling away the moist summer days. The only real tourist site is the church of Nicoya, built in the 1600s. We went to check it out.

It was an old white church. It had big, pale, thick stone walls. The front entrance was open and so we just walked right in. No one else was around. Inside, its ceilings were high and dark. Pigeons fluttered about in the old rafters. There was a misty, hollow feeling. The stone floor was cold. There were a few big windows letting in the tropical sunlight. There were rows of wooden pews and a multitude of various icons and artifacts scattered about the sanctuary. And in the back of the church, in a life-size glass coffin, lay a six-foot-long wooden or plaster statue of Jesus. He was wearing his crown of thorns and most of his body was covered in blood (some kind of red paint). His face expressed grueling agony. After staring at this bloody Jesus for several minutes, I looked up at the surrounding walls and noticed that they were covered in biblical frescoes. All over the walls were various painted murals, muted by time and dust. They were of biblical scenes and characters: the Virgin Mary, Jesus carrying his cross, Abraham about to slaughter Isaac, Joseph and his brothers, the Last Supper, Jacob and Esau, and so on.

And that's when I paused, thought, and turned to my wife: "What is going on? Here we are in a thick rain forest tropical region of Central America, in some tiny village on the Nicoya Peninsula, and these walls are covered with murals depicting ancient Middle Eastern Jews! This bloody Jesus is a Jew from ancient Israel! Mary, Joseph, Jesus, Abraham, Isaac—all Middle Eastern Jews. What the heck are these images, and this statue, doing here?! I mean, Costa Rica has to be as far away from Israel as is possible!"

The answer as to why the church was full of Middle Eastern biblical imagery, and why the vast majority of Costa Ricans are Catholic, has to do with—you guessed it—matters of time and place.

First, we know that the people who originally inhabited Costa Rica for thousands of years prior to the invasion of the Spanish Europeans were not Catholic. They were not any type of Christian at all. They had their own indigenous religious traditions. According to one historical account (Guardia, 1913, 16):

They worshipped the sun, the moon and the elements of nature, personified by the gods of water, fire and the winds. The Bruncas believed that the first man was born of a seed dropped on the earth by an owl sent by God; the Caribs believed that men, animals, and plants alike proceeded from seeds sown by Sibu, the name then and still given by

them to the Supreme Being . . . In the harvest season great religious
festivals were held, at which there were sacrifices, votive offerings,
dances, singing. . . .

So how then do we go from sun and moon worship and seasonal
harvest festivals to the worship of Jesus and Mary? Why is there this
little Catholic church in the middle of the town of Nicoya, decorated
with Middle Eastern characters from thousands of years ago?

Here goes:

About two thousand years ago, a handful of Jews in ancient Israel
began forming various religious groups centered around a Jewish
rabbi by the name of Jesus, whom they believed was the promised
Messiah or some kind of holy/spiritual redeemer. Most Jews back
then did not regard Jesus in such a light, and so those who did were
forced to find converts in the nearby Mediterranean lands, that is,
Syria, Turkey, Cyprus, Malta, southern Italy, and various Greek is-
lands. The "pagans" in these lands began to convert to the growing
Christ-centered religious movements (Christianity). There were
many competing groups and sects of Christians, but the one that
would eventually become dominant (and try its hardest to stamp all
the others out) was what we today would call Catholicism. The
Roman Empire initially persecuted these Catholic Christians. Then,
for reasons that are still debated, the Roman Empire itself, under the
influence and leadership of the Emperor Constantine and then
Theodosius the Great, adopted Christianity as the official state religion in the year 391. Once the Roman Empire adopted Catholicism
as its official religion, wherever the Roman Empire had influence,
Catholicism was also a significant presence.

Spain had been a colony of the Roman Empire since the second
century B.C.E. As soon as the Roman Empire adopted Catholicism as
the official state religion in the fourth century C.E., Catholicism
made serious headway into the Iberian Peninsula. Under the rule of
the Catholic Emperor Theodosius, the long-existing non-Catholic
(pagan) religious traditions in Spain were officially persecuted. Theodosius outlawed all pagan sacrificial rites, both public and private
(Richardson 1998). For some time, paganism still managed to survive
throughout Spain; it is recorded that one civil authority in the year

399 had to halt the government-sanctioned destruction of pagan temples because of popular protest. But after several centuries, Catholicism triumphed (Livermore 1958).

Then, in the 1500s, Spain sent out its representatives across the Pacific to the Americas in search of gold and slaves. One of the places these Spanish conquerors came to in the late sixteenth century was Costa Rica—a Spanish name meaning "Rich Shore." (Rich for whom? Spain, of course.) As a consequence of Spain's brutal conquest of Costa Rica, the population there—those who weren't slaughtered or killed by disease—subsequently became Catholic. Again from Guardia (1913, 10), speaking specifically about the native inhabitants of the Nicoya Peninsula:

> The Nicoya Indians [of the sixteenth century] took their Christianity very seriously . . . their Prince, who called himself Nambi, required that his subjects be referred to as Christians, not Indians. They never rose in revolt and always remained submissive to the Spaniards, which did not prevent the Spaniards, however, from visiting upon them the most cruel treatment and almost completely destroying this intelligent, cultivated and courageous people.

To the contemporary devout Costa Rican Catholic, it may all be a divine story of God's invisible hand guiding his true faith from land to land, from Israel up through the Mediterranean and into Europe and across the great seas all the way to Central America. But to the sociological investigator, it is rather all one long line of arbitrary historical circumstances and random human events. If certain Roman rulers had not adopted Catholicism, it is doubtful Spain ever would have, nor, subsequently, Costa Rica. Or let's say the Roman rulers had adopted Catholicism, but the Roman Empire had never been able to exert such influence over Spain . . . or if it had, but certain Spanish rulers had never decided to send out conquerors across the Pacific in search of gold and slaves . . . or if they had, but these conquerors had not been successful in subduing the native peoples thereof . . . or if—well, you get the idea. The point is that if any one single link of the above historical chain of events had been different, it is safe to say that there would be no bloody Jesus in a small white church in the town of Nicoya today, and Costa Ricans would probably not be so overwhelmingly Catholic today. We could go even further and speculate that had it been Buddhist rulers from Southeast Asia who, in the fifteenth century, decided to send out conquerors across the Pacific in search of gold and slaves, what we now call Costa Rica would most likely have an Asian name, and there would probably be a Buddhist temple in the town of Nicoya, with a statue of a serene Buddha sitting in the back, surrounded by a town and nation full of devout Buddhists.

In short, the sociological exploration of religion reveals that basic factors of time and place are hugely significant in determining the specific religious identity of both individuals and groups.

Take, as one final example: the religiosity of African Americans. Most African Americans are not Jewish or Buddhist or Sikh or Muslim or Hindu or Zoroastrian or Jain or Shinto or Baha'i or even Catholic. The vast majority of African Americans—over 80 percent— are Protestant Christians, predominantly Baptist and Methodist. Why? Without question it is largely explicable by taking the history of the slave trade into account (Raboteau 1999; Baer 1998; Emerson and Smith 2000; Du Bois 2003 [1903]). Most black Americans' ancestors were enslaved by Protestant Christians. The Baptists and Methodists among them made the most concerted effort to spread their particular version of Christianity to the enslaved Africans (Du Bois 2003 [1903]; Washington and Du Bois 1970 [1907]). To be sure, the Protestant Christianity of black Americans is unique, an "Africanized revivalistic Protestantism," to quote Albert Raboteau (1999, 56). Black Christianity was a successful blending of certain versions of white Christianity with many elements of traditional African religion. However, regardless of how "Africanized" it may be, it is still Christianity, with a central emphasis on sin/salvation, heaven/ hell, Jesus, Mary, God, and the Bible.

If we asked randomly selected African Americans why they are Christian, I doubt many would openly declare that it is almost solely because their ancestors were enslaved by Christians. And yet it is un- deniable that the slave trade was a definite/major/decisive factor in the conversion of Africans in North America to Protestant Chris- tianity. It is a fact of history that enraged Malcolm X (1964), for obvious reasons.

Did God allow slavery to occur? Did God guide slavery's development, abetting the white Europeans on their incursions into Africa,
gracing their ships with gentle weather across the Atlantic sea, allowing their centuries of murder, rape, humiliation, family destruction,
and gross exploitation so that the victims would eventually become
Christian? The most successful Protestant evangelical revival preacher
of the eighteenth century, George Whitefield, thought so. When pe-
titioning the British Parliament to allow slavery in the colony of
Georgia, Whitefield argued that God had created the Georgia cli-
mate so as to be just right for blacks to labor and, as a result of their
enslavement, learn the true faith of Christianity, of course (Emerson
and Smith 2000, 26–27).[2]

By discussing the religiosity of Costa Ricans and African Americans,
I have tried to illustrate just how significant matters of time and place
are to individual—as well as group—religious identity. I often lecture
on the contents of this chapter when I teach my course on the sociology
of religion. Inevitably each term, students ask similar questions and
raise similar critiques. I'll close this chapter by summarizing the most
common questions/critiques and by offering my replies.

Student number 1: "But there is so much religious diversity now—
just being from somewhere doesn't mean that you will necessarily be
that area's dominant religion. My uncle is from Mexico, but he isn't
Catholic—he's evangelical Protestant Christian."

This is true. And it is becoming even more true: given the effects
of globalization, mass media, population flows, and shrinking dis-
tances due to advanced transportation systems, just knowing where
someone lives, and when, doesn't mean we can be sure about his or
her religious identity. As Steve Bruce (1999a, 3) comments:

> It used to be possible to guess people's religion from their national-
> ity, region, and class. An eighteenth-century Swede was a Lutheran.
> A ninteenth-century citizen of Cork of native Irish stock was a Roman
> Catholic; if descended from English settlers, an Episcopalian Protes-
> tant. Such regularities are now rare.

Religious diversity is becoming more and more common around
the world, especially here in the United States (Eck 2001; Rourke

1998; Smith 2002). In Los Angeles alone, there are thousands of religions, denominations, sects, and offshoots of probably every tradition imaginable. If you just tell me that you know someone who is "from Los Angeles," it would be next to impossible for me to make a guess as to their religious identity. But if you were to tell me their racial/ethnic identity, class location, where their parents or grandparents are from, what language they speak, and what neighborhood within L.A., then I do think I could still make a very good guess.

Student number 2: "When you speak of Spain conquering Costa Rica and then making the people there Catholic or when you talk about white Europeans or white Americans enslaving Africans and making them Christian, you are arguing that Christianity was just *forced* upon these people. You are implying that they had no choice in the matter. Your analysis does not leave any room for the possibility that maybe Christianity actually spoke to them and meant something to them on a personal, spiritual level."

Guilty as charged. It is true that I am missing something—and skewing the picture—when I describe the religious identities of Costa Ricans and/or African Americans as being solely attributable to conquest and enslavement. Suggesting that native peoples were "forced" into a religion and that it was a completely one-way process (from conqueror/master to conquered/enslaved) is misleading. For one thing, the conquered peoples never completely abandoned their traditional religions outright, but always incorporated vital elements of them into the religion of the Europeans (Raboteau 1978). Furthermore, it must be acknowledged that Christianity did speak to the hearts and souls of the enslaved Africans/Central Americans, despite the malevolent Europeans who "introduced" them to the specifics of the faith. Rodney Stark (1996a) has argued that the growth of Christianity is attributable—more than anything else—to the power and nature of its doctrines. For Stark, the "ultimate factor" (1996, 211) which has led people to accept Christianity is that they have found the religion to be liberating and attractive in and of itself. It is without question that the enslaved Africans and natives of Costa Rica found tremendous hope, comfort, strength, joy, and love in their acceptance of Christianity.

Student number 3: "People do change religions. You said that a child born in Sakakah, Saudi Arabia, today will most likely be

Muslim. But maybe that child will grow up and when she is twenty become a Buddhist."

It is possible, but not likely. Most of us stay the religion in which we were raised (Stark and Finke 2000; Hadaway and Marler 1993). For instance, in the United States, more than 80 percent of us born Catholic stay Catholic, more than 90 percent of us born Protestant stay Protestant, and more than 90 percent of us born Jewish stay Jewish (Greeley 1991). And even if people do choose another religion, they can only choose a religion that crosses their path. They can only switch to a new religion that exists where and when they do and is introduced to them by someone—a friend or missionary—or something—a pamphlet or television show—that intersects with their limited existence. It simply cannot be escaped: time and place are the most unavoidable and salient determinants of religious identity.

Notes

1. The rational choice theorist Laurence Iannaccone (1992, 124) declares that people "approach religion in the same way that they approach other objects of choice. They evaluate its costs and benefits and act so as to maximize their net benefits. Hence they *choose* what religion (if any) they will accept and how extensively they will participate in it." Iannaccone seems to think that people choose their religious identity the same way they choose their toothpaste!

   A major flaw of rational choice theory in general is that the terms it bases itself on (i.e., "rational," "cost," "benefit") are all highly subjective, socially constructed, culturally contested terms. Who is to say what is rational? Since "rational" means dramatically different things to different people, theorizing that people act "rationally" is ultimately meaningless.

   For further discussion of rational choice theory as it applies to religion, suggested work by its proponents includes Young (1997), Stark and Finke (2000), and Iannaccone (1995). Suggested work by its critics include Bruce (1993, 1999a), Bryant (2000), Spickard (1998), Sharot (2002), and Chaves (1995).

2. It should be noted that Africans are not the only people to have been introduced to Christianity under forceful, brutal, unsavory, and all-too-(in)human circumstances. Many whites had similar experiences (Fletcher 1997); King Olav, in the year 1000 C.E., gave his subjects in what is now Norway a choice: convert to Christianity or die! (Palm and Trost 2000).

3

RELIGION IS
SOCIALLY LEARNED

I remember noticing something peculiar when I was only in third grade: all my classmates were the same religion as their parents. All the Jewish kids had Jewish parents. All the Catholic kids had Catholic parents. All the Protestant kids had Protestant parents. And all the kids that "weren't religious" or "didn't have a religion" had parents of the same ilk. And then one day, a young girl named Emily joined our class midyear. What made Emily stand out—or, rather, *sit* out—was that she wouldn't stand and recite the Pledge of Allegiance along with the rest of us each morning. I was completely fascinated by this act of deviance. I thought that it took incredible chutzpah to sit each morning and not stand and recite the Pledge with the rest of the class. In the schoolyard, I quickly found out the reason for Emily's behavior: she was a Jehovah's Witness, and they don't believe in swearing their allegiance to anything but God. And it didn't take me long to find out that—surprise, surprise—Emily's parents were also Jehovah's Witnesses. "So that explains it," I thought to myself as I went to play handball with Stewart Stein.

Looking back now, I like to think that my awareness of parental influence over my fellow third graders' religious identities is evidence that I was simply destined to become a sociologist of religion. By age nine I had already realized a basic premise in the sociological perspective on religion: *it is socially learned*. People learn and acquire their religion from other people (Finney 1978; Chalfant and LeBeff 1991; Batson, Schoenrade, and Ventis 1993, 53).

In any decent introduction to sociology course, professors will spend some time talking about that good old sociological term "socialization."

It gets defined a number of ways, but for me, it simply refers to the process of absorbing the infinite aspects of the culture around us. It is the process of informally learning and unconsciously internalizing the norms, beliefs, and values of our family, peer group, society, nation, and so on. So much of what we know, do, feel, think, and believe comes from how we were/are socialized. In sociology, we refer to the significant and influential people and institutions in our lives—the ones that informally "teach" us our culture—as "agents of socialization." They include parents, friends, relatives, coaches, advertising executives, ministers, baby-sitters, neighbors, teachers, schools, politicians, rock stars, news anchors, and the like. These agents of socialization have an enormously strong and pervasive influence on much of our identities. I could go on and on discussing multiple levels and aspects of socialization, but this isn't the place—and I have already touched upon it in my discussion of Amala and Kamala in chapter 2. The point here is to emphasize that in addition to so many other aspects of ourselves, our religious identities also are often largely a result of basic socialization processes (Fowlkes 1988). Just as we learn our language from others—or what marriage means, or whether eating cow flesh is wonderful or horrible—so too do we learn our religion. More often than not, it is the "significant others" in our lives who play a major role in exposing us to religion and determining our specific religious identities (Batson, Schoenrade, and Ventis 1993).

Let's start with the profound influence the family unit has upon religious identity, particularly parents (Benson, Donahue, and Erickson 1989; Erickson 1992; Mosley and Brockenbrough 1988; Roof and McKinney 1987, 165–166). My experience back in third grade—where all my classmates' religious identities mimicked those of their parents—is quite common, and I would guess similar to the experience of you, the reader. But there are extensive data out there, in addition to our personal recollections. One hundred years ago, in his groundbreaking empirical study of black religious life in the South, W. E. B. Du Bois (2003 [1903]) surveyed over one thousand children and teenagers concerning their religious identity. When asked why they liked a certain church the best over others, the overwhelming majority cited "on account of parents or relatives." For nearly a century since, social scientists have observed the strong correlation between parents and their children in terms of religious identity (Hayes and Pittelkow 1993; Batson, Schoenrade, and Ventis 1993; Hyde 1990; Stark and Glock 1968; Ozorak 1989; Kleugel 1980; Greeley 1982; Hunsberger and Brown 1984; Nelsen 1981; Sherkat and Wilson 1995; Myers 1996). As Argyle and Beit-Hallahmi (1975, 30) conclude, after reviewing extensive literature on the subject, "there can be no doubt that the attitudes of parents are among the most important factors in the formation of religious attitudes." Potvin and Sloane (1985) found that teenagers whose parents are regular church attenders are five times more likely to be religiously active than teenagers whose parents are infrequent or non–church attenders. Stark and Bainbridge (1985) found a significant correlation between parents' beliefs in God and their children's beliefs in God, succinctly concluding that "believers tend to have believers for parents; nonbelievers tend to have nonbelievers for parents" (1985, 330). As cited in the previous chapter, more than 80 percent of Americans born Catholic stay Catholic, more than 90 percent of Americans born Protestant stay Protestant, and more than 90 percent of Americans born Jewish stay Jewish (Greeley 1991). Cornwall (1988) and Stott (1988) looked at Mormon religiosity, finding parental influence on religious identity to be empirically significant, with Stott concluding that his data "clearly support the belief that parents play a dominant role in the religious socialization of their offspring" (1988, 261). Concerning other specific Christian denominations in America, data analyzed and summarized by Spilka, Hood, and Gorsuch (1985) indicate that approximately 75 percent of children born to Baptist parents stay Baptist, approximately 76 percent of children born to Lutheran parents stay Lutheran, and approximately 62 percent of children born to Methodist or Episcopalian parents stay Methodist or Episcopalian, respectively. And it is important to keep in mind that those children who grow up and do not remain in the same specific Christian denomination as their parents will still most likely embrace some other form of Christian religious identity (Hadaway and Marler 1993; Stark and Finke 2000; Bibby and Brinkerhoff 1973; Sherkat 1993).

While the bulk of existing research does support the conclusion that parents clearly influence the religious beliefs and practices of their children, there is debate about the definite strength and actual time span of that influence (Kalish and Johnson 1972; Hoge, Petrillo, and Smith 1982; Bengston 1975; Dudley and Dudley 1986; Francis and Brown 1991). The fact is, of course, that it is not an absolute, air-tight causal relationship. Kids don't always and in every instance automatically adopt the exact same religion as their parents. Far from it. Although changing religions is a rarity in the United States— Stark and Finke (2000, 115) estimate that fewer than 1 percent of Americans convert to a completely new religion—most of us certainly know some people who didn't stick with their parents' religion and grew up to choose different religious paths.

Consider my friend Doug, who wrote that piece on prayer for the introduction to this book. Doug wasn't raised Mormon, but after his marriage to Michelle, he converted to the Church of Jesus Christ of Latter-day Saints. And what is interesting sociologically is that Doug's process of religious conversion/change following his marriage to Michelle is actually quite typical (Musick and Wilson 1995; Alba 1990; Hout and Greeley 1987; Bahr and Albrecht 1989; Hoge 1981). It fits one of the major patterns of religious switching: it is other people in our social world—usually those closest to us—who exert a strong influence over our religious choices/paths (Stark and Bainbridge 1985; Roberts and Davidson 1984; Richardson and Stewart 1977; Gaede 1976). As Stark and Finke (2000, 117) assert, "conversion is seldom about seeking or embracing an ideology; it is about bringing one's religious behavior into alignment with that of one's friends and family members." Our parents are the most influential in influencing our religious identity, as discussed above. And after parents come spouses and friends (Gunnoe and Moore 2002; Stark 1984; Hyde 1990; Willits and Crider 1989; Benson, Donahue, and Erickson 1989; Woodroof 1986; Potvin and Lee 1982; Stott 1988; Lenski 1963; Hoge, Petrillo and Smith 1978). That is, in the rare instances when people don't take on the same religious identity as their parents, they tend to take on the religious identity of their spouse or friends. And if it isn't a parent or spouse or friend, it will probably be a coworker or neighbor who sparks interest in the new faith. In sum, extensive sociological research reveals that people make religious choices and pursue religious paths which tend to follow neatly along lines of preexisting social networks, relational bonds, and personal attachments (Snow and Machalek 1984; Lofland and Stark 1965; Lofland 1966; Kox, Meeus, and t'Hart 1991; Leatham 1997).

All of this can be neatly summed up as follows: we generally acquire and absorb our religion from other people, usually those to whom we are personally close or are significantly attached. And what that ultimately means is that *while religion may have to do with a connection or attachment to God or some other Supreme Reality Out There, more significantly (and observably) it has to do with a connection or attachment to mom or dad or husband or wife or sibling or friend right here on planet Earth.*

Of course, recognizing this fact can be potentially threatening to the deeply religious individual. It suggests that the strong devotion of "Tom" to his religion or Jesus is quite arbitrary; if Tom's social location were different, or if he had had different parents or friends, he most probably would think some other religion was "true" and swear by it with equal passion. This thought always strikes me when I talk with passionate Christians who insist that they would still be Christian even if they had been born in Yemen three hundred years ago. They are so convinced of the eternal truth of their religion that they can't even entertain the notion that had they been born into a different community or country or family at a different time, they would most likely cling to a different religion and be equally convinced of its eternal truth. The fact of the matter is that had Tom been born and raised in Yemen three hundred years ago he would most certainly be a devout Muslim, convinced that Islam and the Qur'an were eternally true, not Christianity and the New Testament. Conversely, if "Mustafa," a devout Wahhabi Muslim of Saudi Arabia—who swears by the truth of the Qur'an and is vehemently certain that Muhammad is the greatest prophet of Allah—had been born and raised in northern Mississippi two hundred years ago, he would most likely be a Baptist or Methodist Christian, safe and secure in his Christian beliefs. Ultimately, religious identity and conviction aren't generally so much a matter of choice or faith or soul-searching as a matter of who and what one's parents, friends, neighbors, and community practice and profess.

It is important to remember that nonbelievers aren't necessarily exempt from this phenomenon, either. After all, I cannot escape the fact that I am a nonbeliever and—surprise, surprise—so are my folks, relatives, and most of my friends. I will be the first to admit that my skeptical agnosticism has its roots clearly in my social environment, and had I been born to devout Sikh parents and lived among other devout Sikhs, I'd most likely be writing a book on the Divine Wisdom and Eternal Truth of the Guru Granth Sahib right now, instead of this little book on the sociology of religion.

But perhaps you aren't convinced about the overwhelming impact of social location on religious identity. Maybe you just aren't sure that religion is so clearly something socially learned from the significant others in our lives. It is quite possible that you just happen to know a real rebel out there, someone who adopted a religion completely on her own. Perhaps your cousin became a pagan witch all by herself, without anyone directly influencing her. She just went out and looked into it, to the surprise and shock of all her friends and family. Such deviant things do happen, however rarely. I'll concede that some people do sometimes choose a religious path completely different from, or even at odds with, the significant others in their social world.

Take the case of John Walker Lindh, the young American found fighting with the Taliban in Afghanistan in the wake of the September 11 terrorist attacks on the United States. John Walker Lindh's parents were Catholic (although his mom, interestingly, converted to Buddhism when John was in adolescence). John had no Muslim relatives, neighbors, or friends, and yet at age sixteen he converted to Islam. On Friday nights, rather than hang out with his friends at the mall or go out on dates, he attended religious services, worshipping at a mosque on the other side of town. After graduating from high school, he left for the Middle East, where he completely committed himself to the study of Islam, roaming from Yemen to Pakistan and eventually up into Afghanistan.

How do we explain John Walker Lindh's religious choice? Clearly he wasn't socialized into Islam by his parents or lured into Islam by a friend or a girlfriend or even a neighbor or coworker. He did take classes on world religions, and his mother did expose him to various religious traditions. But that doesn't explain it. He did read *The Autobiography of Malcolm X*, which apparently got him interested in Islam. But the vast majority of teenagers who read Malcolm X don't convert to Islam. So what exactly was it? The only honest answer: we'll never really know for sure. As Marion Goldman (1999, 216) has eloquently acknowledged, "it is necessary for a blend of personal predispositions and social serendipity to combine at just the right moment in order for someone to join and remain part of a new faith."

But at least this much we can be sure of: his Islamic identity was still *socially learned*. Someone else—some other person or persons—had to teach John Walker Lindh about Islam and show him what it means to be Muslim. Those people may have been strangers from the other side of the city or from faraway lands, but he was still dependent upon other human beings in the formation of his religious identity. Somebody had to tell him about the Qur'an. Somebody had to tell him about the Hadith. Somebody had to tell him about Allah and Mecca and Medina and Muhammad and Ramadan. Someone had to teach him about *shahada, salat, zakat, sawm, Hajj*, and *jihad*. That person may have reached him in the form of a book or pamphlet or television show—but a book or a pamphlet or a television show still originates with somebody, somewhere.

Think about it: the main reason anyone alive today thinks that the Bible is divine (the revealed word of God) is that someone else told them it was. If a hypothetical individual who had never heard of the Bible or its contents found the Bible and read it—if such a person had never been taught about or even heard of God or Moses or Jesus or the Gospels and had never heard of or known of a Jew or a Christian and just found a Bible and read it—there is no reason to suppose that this person would conclude that it was any more holy or profound or divine than the works of Homer, the Tibetan Book of the Dead, the works of J. R. R. Tolkein, the Upanishads, the Qur'an, the Book of Mormon, or the writings of Plato.

Just as factors of time and place greatly affect our religious identities, equally crucial is our social world. We learn our religion—and all its significant particulars—from other people.

As with the contents of the last chapter, whenever I lecture on this chapter's contents, students have typical questions and challenges.

First question: "OK, it is easy to agree that the significant others in our social world teach us many details about religion. Our parents may teach us about the Bible and we probably learn the specific rituals, prayers, and dogmas of our faith from our parents, friends, Sunday school teachers, and so on. But what about people who actually have religious experiences? How can religious experiences be socially learned?"

As discussed in the introduction (see pages 7–9), people do have direct, personal "contacts" with the divine or otherworldly, and these are unavoidably important when trying to understand religion (Davis 1989). Consider this religious experience that a fellow sociologist recently reported to me via e-mail:

> *One day, I went running, and I could see white bands of light that connected the trees to the houses to the grass to the sidewalk to people to dogs and cats walking around, birds flying around, even a few bugs. I have heard things about everything being interconnected, and when I saw these bands of light, I felt that all people were connected with one another, with the animals, with nature, and God, and that these bands were beaming visible manifestations of all of that interconnectedness. I considered this experience deeply spiritual and somehow religious.*

When people claim to have religious experiences, it appears that something manifestly transcendental, mystical, and otherworldly is occurring which must be beyond mere social construction. However, I would still point out that even religious experiences can illustrate the determining influence of social learning. For, if nothing else, religious experiences are clearly socially patterned. Different cultures include within their religious rubric specific "religious experience scripts," and the members of such cultures tend to follow these religious experience scripts quite well, having the exact type of religious experience that is expected in their given culture (Lewis 1971).

Consider the religious experiences which take place in the temple of the goddess Bhadrakali, the patron Hindu deity of Kerala, in southern India (Caldwell 1999). During the *mutiyettu*—the dance-drama-performance offering which is enacted within the temples throughout Kerala—individual participants are believed to actually become possessed by the gods and goddesses, serving as literal human vehicles through which the deities become embodied:

The drums pound relentlessly. The festival of the goddess is in full swing.

Now it is the dead of night. The drama of Bhadrakali and Darika [her enemy] has been unfolding to the deep voices of the drums for several hours. As each scene begins, the actors dance and spin, carefully making offerings of prayers and flowers to the deity . . .

It is the deepest part of the night of the most dangerous day of the week, the time when the ugly and bloodthirsty move abroad in search of their victims. It is a time when people should be safe and asleep in their beds . . . But they are not in their beds. They are here, women, men, and children, in full view of the night sky, the unhealthy mists of evening, the frightening spirits of a Friday night, watching the battle of Bhadrakali and Darika on the dry, barren paddy fields of the village temple grounds. All night the actors and priests have been flirting with the dark powers at large. Everything has been calculated to call forth those powers and to invite them into the performance area, into the person of the actor himself, into the body of the Bhadrakali dancing mutiyettu.

And now it is time. Kali [the goddess] begins to veer madly into the audience, wildly waving her sickle-shaped iron sword in blood lust for Darika's head. People jump up from their seats and run for the safety of the shrine . . . suddenly her heavy head-dress begins to slip, her steps falter, she swoons and begins to tremble violently, her eyes rolling up into her head, her arms flailing. She is helped to her seat near the flame, her head-dress removed, the energy temporarily contained and controlled, her body cooled. (Caldwell 1999, 65).

Consider this typical religious experience from an American Protestant Christian woman who was having doubts about the veracity of her faith (Brasher 1998, 97–98):

One night I said, "Lord if you are real, please reveal yourself to me." I went to sleep with that thought on my mind. The next morning, he woke me up early. I never get up early, but I woke up. There was a rainbow outlining the cross in my room. I have woken up morning after morning, year after year, looking at that cross and there was nothing unusual about it. I did not want to move from that spot. I felt as if I was being bathed in warmth right there. The presence of the Lord was so real and precious at that point that I felt as if I was lying in his arms.

Consider the religious experiences within the rubric of Haitian Vodou, wherein *Gede* spirits or divinities possess and inhabit the bodies of the living (McAlister 2000). As Karen McCarthy Brown (1991, 5) explains:

> Half a dozen times a year . . . Alourdes [a Vodou priestess] holds "birthday parties" for her favorite spirits, or *Iwa*, as they are also called. Clients, friends, and relatives gather around a decorated "niche," whose center-piece is a table laden with food. Here they pray, clap, and sing until the crowd is sufficiently "heated up" to entice a Vodou spirit to join the party, to "ride" Alourdes. In a trance state from which she will later emerge with little or no memory of what has transpired, her body becomes the "horse" of the spirit, her voice the spirit's voice, her words and behavior those of the spirit.

Among certain Christian Holiness religious groups throughout Appalachia, the physical handling of poisonous rattlesnakes can produce religious experiences, as this author recounts of his experience in one such snake-handling church (Covington 1995, 175):

> So I got up there in the middle of the handlers . . . Who was it going to be? Carl's eyes were saying, you. And yes, it was the big rattler, the one with my name on it, acrid-smelling, carnal, alive . . . if I took it, I'd be possessing the sacred . . . This was the moment. I didn't stop to think about it. I just gave in. I stepped forward and took the snake with both hands. Carl released it to me. I turned to face the congregation and lifted the rattlesnake up towards the light. It was moving like it wanted to get up even higher, to climb out of that church and into the air. And it was exactly as the handlers had told me. I felt no fear. The snake seemed to be an extension of myself. And suddenly there seemed to be nothing in the room but me and the snake. Everything else had disappeared. Carl, the congregation, Jim—all gone, all faded to white. And I could not hear the earsplitting music. The air was silent and still and filled with strong, even light. And I realized that I, too, was fading into the white. I was losing myself by degrees, like the incredibly shrinking man . . . I knew then why the handlers took up serpents. There is power in the act of disappearing; there is victory in the loss of self. It must be close to our conception of paradise, what it's like before you're born or after you die . . .

I came back in stages . . . I lowered the snake to waist level. It was an enormous animal, heavy and firm . . . I extended it towards Carl. He took it from me, stepped to the side, and gave it in turn to J.L.

"Jesus," J.L. said. "Oh, Jesus." His knees bent, his head went back. I knew it was happening to him too.

I could go on and on providing examples of various types of religious experiences found within different religious cultures: Native American vision quests, Buddhist meditative experiences, Catholic visions, and so on. But such a catalog of diverse religious experiences from around the world isn't necessary—such experiences need only be broached—to make my argument: social groups and cultures provide the contexts, symbols, triggers, and expectations for the religious experiences their members may have (Yamane and Polzer 1994). Religious experience scripts provide the specific, expected ways to have a religious experience and the contents thereof. Through cultural processes of socialization, people formally or informally learn the religious experience scripts of their culture or religious enclave and subsequently tend to have the exact kinds of religious experiences they are expected to have, in degree, form, shape, and substance. The Hindu worshippers of BhadraKali in Kerela have specific religious experiences involving bodily possession by deities. American Evangelical Protestants have their specific experiences, involving a profound sense of comfort or security and the felt presence of God or Jesus. In a Pentecostal church, speaking in tongues may be the expected experience. Within Haitian Vodou religious culture, bodily possession by spirits is what people expect and experience, with all the behavior and ceremony that go with it. In certain Christian Holiness groups in Appalachia, snake handling comes with its specific form of religious experience. In sum, though we can't write off religious experiences as being pure social constructions—something otherworldly may very well be occurring—we can still be sociologically confident that social learning is always a key ingredient and a determining, filtering factor. Even in the midst of dramatically personal and spiritual experiences of the otherworldly, cultural patterns and societal expectations are perpetual determining forces.

And now for the second common question that usually arises from students concerning religion being socially learned:

"Even though people obviously learn a lot about religion from those around them, this doesn't account for the genesis of a new religion. What about the people who start new religions? If you are arguing that we just learn our religion from others, well, then, how does the religion we are learning start in the first place? John Walker Lindh may have been taught about Islam by other people—but how did Islam originate? How do sociologists explain the birth of new religions?"

My first response to this important line of questioning is to begin by reminding students that successful new religions are excruciatingly rare. Sure, new religious groups pop up all the time, but how many of them actually flourish for multiple generations? How many new religions actually survive the death or disgrace of their charismatic leader? And of those that do, how many last more than one or two hundred years? The truth is, the overwhelming majority of new religions die relatively quickly. As Armand Mauss (1994, viiii) acknowledges, "history suggests that the overwhelming majority of [religious] movements fail to survive even one generation, to say nothing of enduring across the centuries." Of the religions that seem to have "made it" and are currently thriving on the planet, many don't have actual historical founders that we can point to (Hinduism, for instance). Some religions do have known historical founders, but these individuals are mind-numbingly rare. Just think of how many people have ever lived on this earth. Billions and billions. Now, of all the people who have ever lived, how many have started successful new religions? Twelve? Twenty? More than 99.99 percent of humanity doesn't found a successful new religion. So by arguing that religion is socially learned, that is, that people learn their religion from other people (which is the whole point of this chapter), I believe I am accurately accounting for the religious identities/experiences of more than 99.99 percent of humanity.

"But it does happen," the student rebuts. "Individuals do construct new religious traditions. You are avoiding the question."

My second response is to then remind students that "new" is a very relative and even questionable term when discussing the development of religious traditions. The fact is, every successful new religious tradition grows within a specific sociohistorical context, and thus unavoidably develops out of a preexisting religious culture. This means that every "new" religious tradition borrows from, reiterates, reinterprets, reflects, and straight-out plagiarizes from the religion or religions that have come before it. For instance, Christianity elaborates upon preexisting Judaism, Islam draws from preexisting Judaism and Christianity, Mormonism elaborates upon long-established Judaism and Christianity, Baha'ism grows out of Islam, Sikhism develops out of preexisting Hindu and Islamic traditions, and so on. OK, I'm still avoiding the question. The fact is, qualitatively new religions *do* arise, despite their dependence on preexisting traditions.

But I also can't help pointing out to students that in many instances of individuals starting new religions, the first converts to the new tradition are invariably family members and friends of that individual (Stark 1999)! The first converts to Islam were Muhammad's family and friends. The first converts to Mormonism were Joseph Smith's family and friends (Persuitte 2000). This further illustrates the importance of preexisting social relationships in (new) religious identities.

So when asked about the emergence of new religions I point out that (1) the successful creation of new religions is extremely rare, (2) no religion is completely "new," as all religions develop from preexisting religions, and (3) conversion to new religions seems to follow preexisting social networks. But I am still avoiding the ultimate question: How do we sociologically explain the birth of new religions?

I think most social scientists and historians of religion would subscribe to a sort of "right person, right time, right place" theory. This runs as follows: a highly motivated and inspired individual arises (such as Muhammad or Joseph Smith) who possess an abundance of charisma—a magnetic personal character trait made sociologically famous by Max Weber (1978). This individual formulates a clear religious vision which strongly resonates with the people receiving it on a variety of levels: psychologically, politically, economically, aesthetically, and, of course, theologically. The social circumstances are thus that the new religious vision is somehow able to grow and spread, despite persecution. And then, even after the disappearance of the remarkable individual who started it all, the tradition continues as a result of sound leadership, carefully crafted scriptures, and meaningful traditions and rituals. To be sure, sociologists and historians of religion have written and debated every single aspect of the above scenario, in abundance (Weber 1946; Moore 1986; Stark 1987; Wilson 1987; Bird 1993; Hammond and Machacek 1993; Miller 1991; Johnson 1992). But the overall point of this theoretical perspective is to assert that the emergence of successful new religions has to do with an exceedingly rare convergence of specific historical, personal, political, psychological, cultural, and theological circumstances.

In the end, the sociologist must also allow for the possibility that he or she simply can't explain everything. The sociological observer of religion must admit that maybe, just maybe, the founder of a new religion is indeed actually serving as a channel or voice or vehicle for the divine/otherworldly. Despite the lack of reliable data, we must entertain the possibility that when Muhammad recited the Qur'an, he really actually and literally was acting as the mouthpiece for Allah. Or when Joseph Smith was composing the Book of Mormon, he really was truly translating divinely inspired words. Or when Ann Lee of the Shakers was spreading her teachings, or when Paul was writing his epistles, or when the authors of the Upanishads were at work, they were actually and truly operating as loudspeakers for that great, mystical stereo in the sky. Personally, I think discerning whether such is the case is a matter of empirical evidence. Others, no doubt, would argue that it is a matter of personal faith. You will have to decide that one for yourself (but be forewarned: the significant others in your social world will most likely influence your decision!).

4

RELIGION OR CULT?

Whenever I teach my sociology of religion class, one of my assignments is to have students go out into the "real world" and participate in, carefully observe, and then write a report about a religious service not of their own tradition. For some students, especially those who have never attended a religious gathering before, it can be a terrifying experience. They fear that they will stick out or be stared at or somehow be awkwardly ostracized as an unwelcome outsider, an obvious nonbeliever, or worse yet—an interloping spy from a sociology class! Usually, nothing happens to my fearful students other than that they end up meeting very friendly people or hearing beautiful music or tasting bland wafers or listening to provocative sermons or overhearing typical daily-life chitchat, and ultimately learning a bit about how contemporary Americans worship.

Sally and Ted were both in my class a couple of years ago. They each went out on their own to observe a church service of a religious denomination that they had had no previous connection with. And they were both exasperated by what they experienced.

Sally came to my office one Monday morning, wanting desperately to discuss her experience. She told me the following:[1] "Oh, my goodness, Professor Zuckerman. My observation experience was freaky! What a weird and strange religion! I went to their house of worship and was there for the whole service and all I can say is that it was really disturbing. Everyone felt like they were all mindless zombies! People just stood up and down on cue like robots, mindlessly repeating words over and over again in unison. There was no joy on anyone's face. They were all so stiff and deadpan. And the leader would say these weird, monotone words and then everyone would all just repeat things back to him in unison and without any feeling. Like they were brainwashed. No one seemed alive. They all felt totally programmed. It was like they were just doing everything out of some sort of memorized repetition. It was really, really weird. I swear, *it felt like a cult!*"

Sally was describing a Catholic mass at a local Catholic church in town. Sally had grown up in an evangelical-charismatic, nondenominational Protestant congregation and, to her, this traditional Catholic style of worship was cultlike.

But wait—here's what Ted had to tell me about his experience only a few days later:[2]

"Professor Zuckerman—my observation experience was totally bizarre! It really freaked me out! I went to the building and was there for several hours. Everything was so chaotic. People were literally screaming and singing out and shouting all over the place almost the entire time. It felt like spiritual mayhem. The preacher was sweating and prancing about the stage for an hour, yelling and howling, while people shouted randomly back at him the whole time. Lots of people had their arms over their heads during the service, with their hands open like they were feeling warm light on their palms or something. When they sang they would hold their hands high and sway them back and forth—like at a rock concert. Many of them would sing with their eyes closed and with this weird smile—it felt like a Grateful Dead show or something. And then at one point some people started mumbling in this strange way—making weird, incomprehensible sounds like they were in a trance or something. One woman behind me fell down mumbling with her eyes rolling back—I thought she was having an epileptic seizure or something! But people just sort of acted like it was no big deal. There was a lot of energy, but it felt scary. People just seemed like they were on drugs or under a spell. I swear, *it felt like a cult!*"

Ted was describing an evangelical-charismatic, nondenominational Protestant service at a local church in town. Ted had grown up Catholic and, to him, this exuberant style of worship was cultlike.

The point of all this should be obvious: *one person's religion is another person's cult*. And that is exactly what I say whenever I am at a party, standing by the chips and guacamole, sipping my beverage, talking to somebody about what I do. The conversation usually runs as follows:

New acquaintance says: "So my company . . . *blah,blah,blah* . . . and what do you do?"

"I teach at a small liberal arts college . . . *blah, blah, blah* . . . so, yeah, I'm a sociologist of religion."

"Oh, really? That's fascinating. Say, what do you think of those Zen meditation people—they're a cult, right?" *Note*: for "Zen meditation people" one could easily insert just about any religion. I've heard Catholics, Hasidic Jews, Scientologists, Mormons, Baptists, Muslims, Sikhs, Buddhists, Jehovah's Witnesses, Baha'is, Seventh-Day Adventists, and a whole slew of other religious organizations referred to as "cults" by various people in the course of various similar conversations. And in most instances, what people seem to be wanting me to say is, "Oh sure, they are definitely a cult, and they are really weird. Take it from me, I'm a scholar, an expert. You don't want your son/daughter/boyfriend/mother-in-law associating with them!"

Instead, much to the disappointment of my new acquaintance, I shrug my shoulders and say that I don't really use the word "cult"— that is has very little meaning for me as a sociologist of religion and that, well, *one person's religion is another person's cult*. At that point, the topic of conversation either switches to the weather, or my new acquaintance starts in on me about cults: "How can you say there are no such things as cults? Surely cults are not the same thing as *real* religions!"

What is so fascinating to me is that, at root, the whole issue concerning whether this or that group is a "cult" or a "religion" is an excellent example of the social construction of religious legitimacy versus religious illegitimacy.

The first question, of course, is: What does the term "cult" actually mean? What makes one group a religion and another group a cult? What do these commonly thrown around terms such as "cult," "sect," "denomination," "religion" actually signify? Unfortunately, the disappointing fact is that these terms are not empirically derived descriptions of static phenomena. Rather, they are malleable, contested, and ever-changing social constructs. Don't misunderstand me: there is a long, rich, and respectable history in the sociology of religion of defining and substantiating these terms in a deliberate, scholarly manner (Troeltsch 1931; Johnson 1963, 1971; Swatos 1981; Bainbridge

1997; Stark and Bainbridge 1985; Wilson 1993; Zablocki and Robbins 2001). But the definitions that scholars concoct, while intelligent, sound, and theoretically useful, are not the definitions that most people are familiar with (Richardson 1993b; Richardson and van Driel 1997). For most people, the term "cult" is essentially a pejorative label used to deprecate or delegitimize a given group (Bromley and Hadden 1993, 6). The term "religion," on the other hand, is basically a label designating acceptance and respect, or at least denoting legitimacy. And depending on whether the one doing the describing wants to put down and insult a group or respect and support a group, they'll use whichever word suits their given ideological, political, or theological purposes. Thus, regardless of what we academics may declare in our journal articles and conference presentations, my general sense is that for most contemporary Americans, these terms mean the following:

- A *cult* is a small religious group that is bizarre at best, deadly at worst. Cults are something to be suspicious of. They are dangerous and certainly not "legitimate" religious organizations.
- A *sect* resembles a cult—small and kind of weird, different, perhaps troublesome—but is not as bad, bizarre, or dangerous. Sects may or may not be "legitimate" religious groups; their status is somewhat borderline.
- A *denomination* is just a subsection of a larger religion, and is generally considered a legitimate religious body.
- A *religion* is a large religious group that is unquestionably legitimate.

Again, these are *not* the definitions that professional scholars of religion subscribe to. They are rather definitions which merely reflect my personal sense of what people out in the world think of and say when they hear or use these terms.

So now back to my conversation over chips and guacamole. My new acquaintance is disgruntled by my not agreeing that this or that group should be labeled a cult, and he is even more curious/annoyed as to how I can just completely write off the term "cult" itself. So I ask him what makes a group a cult, and he rattles off various typical characteristics and selected phenomena people commonly associate with cults. I then proceed to explain that these characteristics can be found all over the religious map and can be associated with just about any religious tradition/organization at one time or another, to one degree or another.

Here, then, are the more common associations people have with cults, along with my discussion of how they are not so strictly limited, that they can often apply to the most "noncultlike" religions.

First is the notion that *cults are religious groups led by a charismatic leader*. Surely when people think of cults, they think of masses of adherents pledging their allegiance to some single powerful individual. They think of followers devoting their souls and wallets to some head honcho, powerful guru, master, or supposed prophet. These devotees willingly submit to his or her authority, soulfully abide by his or her decisions, dutifully obey his or her rules and guidelines. They look to this charismatic leader for wisdom, spiritual counsel, enlightenment. They accept and value his or her insights concerning not only the cosmos but mundane aspects of their daily lives. This leader is seen as personally holy. He or she is somehow closer to the Divinity—maybe even a direct spokesperson for the Divinity. Maybe even God incarnate. Such a leader can be found among many religious organizations that people might consider to be cultlike. We can immediately think of Bagwan Sri Rajneesh and his group of followers (the "Rajneeshies"). Or David Berg and The Family/Children of God. Or Elizabeth Clair Prophet and Church Universal Triumphant. Or the Reverend Sun Myung Moon and the Moonies/ Unification Church. But—and here's where I try to sock it to my party friend—we could also throw in Roman Catholicism! After all, if there ever was a charismatic leader who held sway over his faithful followers and was considered by many to be holy/close to the Divinity and whose teachings and insights are granted sacred weight and whose very being commands holy reverence, it would be the pope. And yet surely most people don't think of Roman Catholicism—the single largest Christian denomination in the world, with hundreds of millions of followers—as a cult.

What religion hasn't at one time or another been under the leadership of a strong, powerful, charismatic figure who demanded unfailing allegiance and personal sacrifices of his or her followers? It could be argued that Islam—the second-largest religion in the world today— began as a "cult" around Muhammad. The Church of Jesus Christ of Latter-day Saints began as a "cult" around Joseph Smith. And the list goes on and on: Bahu'u'allah and the Baha'is, John Knox and Presbyterians, Martin Luther and/or John Calvin and their Protestant Christian progeny, Guru Nanak and the Sikhs, The Ba'al Shem Tov and Hasidic Judaism, Charles Taze Russell and Jehovah's Witnesses, Mary Baker Eddy and Christian Science, Ellen Gould White and the Seventh-Day Adventists, Emanuel Swedenborg and Swedenborgianism, John Wesley and Methodism, George Fox and the Quakers, Aimee Semple McPherson and the Foursquare Gospel Church, Ernest Holmes and Religious Science.[3] And many religious bodies today continue to be led by charismatic or authoritative or divinely inspired leaders, including Roman Catholicism (as mentioned above), various Jewish Hasidic sects, Sikhs, The Nation of Islam, Mormons—again, the list goes on and on. In sum, virtually every major, "legitimate" religion today was at one time—or continues to be—led by a charismatic leader.

A second association people have with "cults" is *brainwashing*. Many people believe that cults are religious groups that somehow have the mysterious ability to brainwash unsuspecting, gullible members through some rigorous and perfected method of psychological "mind control" (Bromley and Hadden 1993, 30). As has already been discussed in chapter 1 (see page 28), sociological research has revealed that there is simply no such thing as brainwashing. We have no empirical proof that people can systematically and tactically control the minds of others to get them to do or believe things explicitly against their will (Robbins 1984).

Of course, people can be manipulated. People can be swayed, cajoled, coaxed, seduced, deceived, duped, pressured, pushed, prodded—just go out and try buying a new car! There are certainly religious groups out there that apply social-psychological pressures on their members to conform, or to accept hard-to-swallow beliefs, or to make monetary or emotional sacrifices. But you will find these same mechanisms at play in an army boot camp. Or in your own family. The fact of the matter is that social-psychological manipulation and

dynamics of social pressure are commonplace and abundant, permeating endless arenas of our social world: in the military, in college
dormitories, in high school friendship cliques, in business environments, in education, in politics, in sex, in advertising, in sports, in the
courtroom, in the family, in fraternities, in the workplace, and so on.
And more important, one can observe that various forms of social-
psychological manipulation are a typical ingredient in almost any
mainstream or "legitimate" religious tradition. Children in almost
every "legitimate" religion are socially and psychologically pressured
into accepting all sorts of beliefs and engaging in all sorts of activities
they wouldn't necessarily choose on their own were it not for the
guiding force they experience (often unconsciously) from their parents, friends, and teachers. And yet isn't it interesting that when a
twenty-year-old joins the Hare Krishnas, people suspect he has been
brainwashed, but no one speaks of sending five-year-old children to
Sunday school as brainwashing. And yet who is more susceptible to
psychological manipulation? Who has less life experience and intellectual capacity to measure truth from falsehood? Who is more likely
to succumb to the influence of teachers and peers: the twenty-year-
old on the streets of San Francisco or the five-year-old in Sunday
school? Without question, the five-year-old. As Catherine Wessinger
(2000, 6) has observed:

> The "cult" stereotype conveys the belief that members of unconven-
> tional religions are "brainwashed." The brainwashing theory provides a
> simplistic explanation of why people adopt strange beliefs that are un-
> believable to members of mainstream society. The brainwashing theory
> overlooks the fact that mainstream social and religious institutions also
> indoctrinate and socialize people. Children are indoctrinated in Sunday
> and church schools, in catechism classes, and by homeschooling. Indi-
> viduals attending military schools are socialized in brutal hazing pro-
> cesses . . . We are all socialized by our parents, teachers, ministers,
> friends, spouses, and peers . . . the processes utilized by members of
> NRMS [New Religious Movements/cults] are not different from those
> used in mainstream families and institutions.

Again, while we can acknowledge that social-psychological manipulation does take place in various religious circles—and that some

religious leaders or organizations may be qualitatively better at it than others—this does not mean that certain religious groups have mastered a mysterious, proficient form of mind manipulation and that they have it down to such an exact science that they can get people to do or believe things completely against their will to a degree unparalleled by other religious communities.

A third common phenomenon that people associate with "cults" is that *they urge their members to do illegal, criminal, or murderous acts*. We can immediately think of Jim Jones and his Peoples Temple and their suicide/murder of nearly a thousand people in Guyana in 1978. Or of David Koresh and his Branch Davidians and the deadly inferno in Waco, Texas, in 1993. Or of Shoko Asahara and his Aum Shinrikyo movement of Japan, responsible for gassing subways in Tokyo in 1995. Or the suicide of thirty-five members of the Heaven's Gate group in San Diego in 1997. While some contemporary religions clearly engage in murderous or criminal activities, an even cursory perusal of the history of nearly all major "legitimate" religions will reveal that they too, at one time or another, have exhibited morbid, unethical, brutal, and/or suicidal tendencies (Juergensmeyer 2001). Judaism, Islam, Catholicism, Protestant Christianity, Hinduism, Sikhism—all of these religions have had periods in their history in which violence and/or lawbreaking and/or seemingly unethical or apparently self-destructive conduct was expected, condoned, deemed holy, and actively engaged in by various adherents and leaders. Thus, designating a religious body as "cultlike" because some of its members or leaders engage in criminal, bloody, or suicidal activity is historically blind; again, almost all religions, at one time or another, have done the same.

A fourth and final association people have concerning "cults" is that *they have weird beliefs*. Consider the Raelians, whose charismatic leader—a former French journalist and race car driver named Claude Vorilhon, also known as Rael—claims to have had contact with aliens. According to Raelian belief, humans were created by alien scientists and we are soon approaching the time when our alien creators will return to earth.[4] While such beliefs may strike one as odd, an unbiased perusal of the foundational beliefs of almost every religion will reveal equally bizarre or weird tenets. The unavoidable sociological bottom line when studying religions is that what constitutes beliefs as "weird" is always a matter of subjective opinion. I may think Scientologists have weird beliefs. But Scientologists may think Baha'is have weird beliefs, and Baha'is may think Lutherans have weird beliefs, and Lutherans may think Wiccans have weird beliefs, and Wiccans may think Muslims have weird beliefs, and it just goes on and on and on. Again, from Wessinger (2000, 5):

> The comparative study of the world's religions shows that beliefs and practices that are regarded as strange in one religion are normative in another. For instance, Hindus and Buddhists believe in reincarnation, while reincarnation is viewed by most Christians as an unusual belief associated with "cults." Conversely, Christians believe that Jesus's resurrection from the dead is true, but this doctrine is viewed by members of other religions as fantastic and unbelievable.

The very word "weird"—like "beautiful" or "deviant" or "successful" or "rational"—is one that has no empirical, scientific foundation, but only subjective, socioculturally determined meanings that are ever-changing and ever-contested.

In sum, the supposedly unique or distinguishing characteristics people associate with religious organizations they wish to delegitimize by labeling them as "cults"—charismatic leadership, brainwashing, destructive behavior, weird beliefs—can be found in almost any religion in one way or another, to one degree or another, or at one time or another, rendering the whole distinction between "cult" and "religion" intellectually indefensible.

Despite my protests outlined above, most people out there are still going to differentiate between "religions" and "cults." Most people are still going to use terminology to put down some religious groups, while supporting (legitimizing) others. My fascination is to try to understand how and in what ways this plays itself out. And I believe that it has little or nothing to do with the actual content of the organization's beliefs, rituals, or structure.

In listening to the way people talk about religions/cults, in watching the way the media depict and discuss religions/cults, in observing how religious groups are accepted or denounced in political and other cultural arenas, and in studying religious sociohistorical dynamics, I've come to the conclusion that the social construction of religious legitimacy generally boils down to two basic factors: (1) the amount of time the religious group has been in existence and (2) the sheer number of members involved.

First, the time factor. The longer a religious group exists, the less likely it is going to be characterized as a "cult" and the more likely it will be accepted as a legitimate religion. Whenever new religious movements first arrive on the scene, they are often regarded suspiciously, especially by other religions. But in time, if they aren't snuffed out, they become more and more accepted. For example, there was a time in British history when being a Quaker was synonymous with being a social and theological criminal, a deviant religious outlaw. Quakers were ruthlessly persecuted. And yet, over time, Quakerism became accepted as a respectable and even benign religious organization. Or another example: the Church of Jesus Christ of Latter-day Saints—Mormons. There was a time in this country when being a Mormon was synonymous with being a social and theological criminal, a deviant religious outlaw. Mormons suffered extensive persecution and violence at the hands of those who considered them a dangerous and illegitimate religious organization. And yet today, most Americans view Mormonism as just another established religion—after all, we have elected representatives in the House and the Senate who are Mormons. In short, the sheer passing of time seems somehow to confer religious legitimacy. The group's beliefs can remain virtually the same, the style of worship can remain the same, the leadership hierarchy can stay in place, the basic raison d'être of the religious group need not alter. The group just needs to stick around long enough, and societal acceptance will eventually result.[5]

A second factor in the construction of religious legitimacy involves nothing more than numbers. I call it the numbers rule of religious legitimacy. It goes like this: If one lone individual firmly believes in something that no one else believes in (and for which there is little or no empirical evidence), people generally call such an individual "insane" or "crazy." Now, if, say, ten or fifty people firmly believe in something that no one else believes in (and for which there is little or no empirical evidence), people might refer to such a group as a "cult."

But if five hundred or five thousand people firmly believe in something which no one else believes in (and for which there is little or no empirical evidence), such a group might be referred to as a "sect." And if the number gets up into fifty thousand or maybe five hundred thousand then we're talking "denomination." And if the numbers are, say, five million or more, we've got ourselves a bona fide "religion." Of course, I am picking these numbers arbitrarily. The point I am simply trying to make is that religious legitimacy often boils down to how many people are members of a given organization, and nothing more.

This can also be seen in the use of the word "myth" versus the designation of "religious narrative." The use of these words/descriptive labels plays into the whole social construction of religious legitimacy/illegitimacy. A myth commonly means something that isn't factually true, a folk legend, an old tale, a story that isn't really historically accurate. We often speak of Greek myths or Native American myths, implying that these ancient and fantastical descriptions of the world's origins and various gods and goddesses are clearly and enjoyably fictitious. But people seldom if ever speak of Jewish myths or Buddhist myths or Christian myths. Why? What makes one ancient, fantastical tale a "myth" and yet another equally ancient and fantastical tale a "religious narrative" whose factuality cannot be questioned? Again, it all boils down to numbers. A "myth" is simply a religious narrative without any sizable number of people believing in its historical validity anymore. The ancient Jewish/Christian story of the earth's origin (as described in Genesis of the Bible) and the ancient Sumerian story of the earth's origin are both equally "mythological" and manifestly unbelievable from an empirical point of view. And yet one is deemed a religious narrative and the other a myth. Why? Because one has millions of people believing it as truth and the other doesn't.

Of course, there are multiple factors which are at play in the social construction of the legitimacy or illegitimacy of a given religious organization, beyond the two I have highlighted, time and numbers. We could speak of power; often the labeling of a group as a cult comes down to who in a given society has the power to do such labeling, that is, the government, the media, or professors of religion. And it is crucial to remember that each religious movement has its own particular story embedded in its own particular sociohistorical context, the details of which would require careful study to understand how the designation as cult or religion occurs in that specific instance. And finally, it is crucial to recognize that the labels "religion" and "cult" are often nebulous and seldom fixed; for example, while most Americans seem to accept Mormonism as a legitimate religion, there are certainly those who still would label it a cult. And there are many religious organizations that tread a fine line between cult and religion, hovering precariously between societal acceptance and suspicion, between religious legitimacy and illegitimacy—for instance, Scientology (Aldrige 2000; Stark and Bainbridge 1985).

Scientology is currently waging an international public relations campaign to disassociate itself from the label "cult" and gain acceptance as a "real" religion, for a variety of reasons—legal, financial, and otherwise. I was recently sent a big, handsome, hard-back book (unsolicited) by the Church of Scientology International; the chapters and appendices are devoted to "proving" that Scientology is a "real" religion. And the stakes are quite high for Scientologists. If they are deemed a "real religion" by those in power, they can enjoy everything from tax breaks to societal respect. But if they are deemed a "cult," they risk lawsuits, legal persecution, and societal rejection. In the case of Scientology, it may not be sheer numbers of adherents or time in existence that establishes its legitimacy but savvy public relations and successful lawyers.

Personally, having read *Dianetics* and having gone through some elementary Scientology therapy and having studied the beliefs and practices of the movement, I find its truth claims about this world and beyond, its basic philosophies and teachings, and its common techniques in human betterment uninviting and rather dubious. To put it simply, I don't buy it. But I also personally have no reason or need to label them a "cult." And as a sociologist, I am certain that such a designation is ultimately meaningless.

"But they take lots of money from their members!" says my aggravated acquaintance standing by the chips and guacamole.

"What religious organization doesn't?" I reply. "My Baptist in-laws give 10 percent of their income to their church. It would cost me $2,000 a year to belong to my local synagogue!"

"But they have really weird beliefs! And their whole thing was founded by this charismatic leader who just manipulated people, and they brainwash their members . . ."

"Yeah, *whatever.*"

And that's when I excuse myself to go outside for a breath of fresh air.

Notes

1. I didn't record the conversation, and am thus paraphrasing her words from memory. However, her concluding sentence (about their being a cult) is accurately etched in my brain.
2. Again, I am paraphrasing from memory.
3. Even though it could be argued that the New Testament portrays early Christianity as a "cult" around the charismatic leadership of Jesus, I am not including Jesus or Christianity in my list above because a substantial and growing body of scholarship has successfully called into question the historical accuracy of the New Testament, particularly concerning the biographical details of the character Jesus (Doherty 2000, 2001; Helms 1988; Wells 1975, 1988; Price 2000; Leidner 1999; Freke and Gandy 1999; Ellegard 1999). The same goes for Buddha and Buddhism (Price 1999). Additionally, the accurate historical origins of Hinduism and Judaism are too obscure to be certain of any specific charismatic leader(s).
4. See www.rael.org for more information.
5. This discussion directly relates to why many sociologists of religion prefer to use the designation "new religious movement" instead of "cult." Aside from recognizing that "cult" has a derogatory ring which the term "new religious movement" avoids, use of this designation implicitly acknowledges that the "novel" or "odd" aspect of the given organization is really only a result of its limited time on the scene (i.e., being a *new* religion) , and nothing more.

5

SOCIAL LIFE
AFFECTING RELIGION

In 1903, W. E. B. Du Bois's literary and sociological classic *The Souls of Black Folk* was published. The book is a personal, poetic, and piercing collection of essays concerning various aspects of American life in the post–Civil War United States, with a particular focus on matters of race. Chapter 12, "Of Alexander Crummel," recalls the true story of a young man who felt called to live a devoted religious life. Crummel was a brilliant, eloquent, contemplative individual with an unyielding passion to do the Lord's work, to preach the Good News, and to lead others in Christian living. There was only one problem: he was black. When he sought to enter the seminary in order to be ordained, the veil of racism came quickly cascading down, as the "calm, good men, Bishops of the Apostolic Church of God . . . [declared that] . . . the General Theological Seminary of the Episcopal Church cannot admit a Negro" (Du Bois 1989 [1903], 155).

Alexander Crummel's experiences of racism in his religious strivings were far from unique. On the contrary: such experiences were all too common. Yes, even in the realm of religion, in that realm of human intercourse presumably formed around and devoted to love and goodwill, the poison of racism can seep deeply and widely. This fact didn't go unnoticed by Du Bois. In an essay written in 1929 titled "The Color Line and the Church," he characterized Christianity in America as being "Jim Crowed from top to bottom. No other institution in American is built so thoroughly or more absolutely on the color line" (quoted in Weinberg 1970, 216). The reason racism was such a pernicious ingredient of religious life in America one hundred years ago is simple: racism was a pernicious ingredient of

American society in general. As Du Bois explained, "White Americans prefer not to associate with Negroes, neither in homes, theaters, streetcars nor churches" (quoted in Weinberg 1970, 216). And such racial segregation in virtually all aspects of social as well as religious life is still remarkably widespread in America today (Emerson and Smith 2000; Hacker 1995; Massey and Denton 1993; Lincoln 1984).

The point of all this is not to criticize American Christianity for its historical and contemporary failings concerning racial integration. Rather, I use this example provided by Du Bois of racism in American religious life to make a larger, more theoretical point which is crucial to the sociological study of religion: religious life will always be enmeshed in and affected by whatever sociocultural winds are blowing in, through, and past its midst. Because racism has pervaded much of American society, so too will racism pervade much of American religion. It is inevitable.

Religion must be understood and studied not as a separate reality/entity unto itself. Rather, is must be recognized that religion is always enmeshed within a specific sociocultural environment. Social forces, human institutions, and cultural productions perpetually inform, determine, and shape religious experiences and institutions. Gender norms, sexualities, political debates, economic phenomena, racial matters, ecological circumstances, media forces, family structures, technological developments, artistic movements—anything and everything that is significant in social life in general will also be significant in religious life. Whether reinforcing or refusing, abetting or battling, lauding or decrying, religion is always and in every historical instance in an inextricable dance with the specific social norms, values, symbols, and institutions of the broader culture within which it dwells.

Of course, religion never simply reacts. Religion is never just a passive partner in the dance. If society or culture can be compared to a cake made up of various ingredients, religion is often a key ingredient in the sociocultural batter, adding its particular flavor and spice and subsequently affecting all the other ingredients and greatly determining the overall composition of the cake. Although much of what sociologists do is study the ways in which other social factors affect religious life, we are always cognizant of the fact that religious experiences and institutions in turn perpetually inform, determine, and shape other elements of society as well. It is ultimately this dialectic—how various social phenomena affect religious life and how religious life in turn affects other social phenomena—which fascinates sociologists of religion.

This chapter will look at one side of the dialectic: social life affecting and influencing religious life. I'll offer two illustrations. First, an example of race matters influencing religious life as observed in the case of the development of specific Mormon doctrines and practices. For a second example, I will consider feminism's impact on American religious life, drawing specifically from my own research on a Jewish community in Oregon.

When most people think of Mormons, they tend to think of either polygamy or coffee, the former being condoned and the latter forbidden. However, this is only 50 percent correct. Although the largest denomination of Mormonism—the Church of Jesus Christ of Latter-day Saints, based in Utah—fiercely defended polygamy in its earliest decades, it condemned the practice in the 1890s and has ever since strongly advocated monogamy as the solely acceptable form of marriage (Hardy 1992; Hansen 1981; Ivins 1972).[1] As for the avoidance of coffee—and all "hot drinks" in general—that is still in effect (Doctrines and Covenants 89:9).

Though the process through which Mormons came to abandon polygamy and the reasons why they continue to avoid hot beverages are both fascinating topics, I'll be exploring another aspect of Mormonism: its racist past. The story of how Mormonism developed throughout the nineteenth century as an overtly racist religious movement and subsequently evolved into a more racially open, tolerant, and accepting religious organization in the last few decades neatly and almost perfectly illustrates the theoretical argument of this chapter: that what is going on "out there" in the social world often seeps into religious life, whether the religious participants themselves care to admit it or not.

Before I proceed, let me state explicitly that I am not saying Mormonism began as an intentionally, uniquely, or wholly racist religion or that all early Mormons were racists. Such a position would be ridiculously myopic and historically untenable. In the early decades of its development, Joseph Smith and other Mormon leaders often denounced slavery. Also, the Book of Mormon contains some explicitly universalistic passages in which both "black and white" are welcomed unto the Lord (II Nephi 26:33). And though their numbers were exceedingly miniscule, there were a handful of black members of the Mormon Church in its earliest days (Embry 1994). One such early black Mormon was Elijah Abel, who joined in the 1830s, when the religion was in its infancy. He played an active leadership role in Mormon affairs and was a close associate of Joseph Smith's. However, despite granting the above facts, I would still classify the character of most of Mormonism's history as one leaning more toward racism than not (see Bringhurst 1981).

I first became conscious of Mormonism's awkward handling of race matters when I picked up and read the most holy of Mormon scriptures, the Book of Mormon.[2] Some things immediately stood out for me. For instance, God turns people's skin black when they do bad things against his will (II Nephi 5:21). Those who lack faith in the God of Mormonism are turned into "dark and loathsome . . . filthy people" (I Nephi 12:23). Sin is explicitly associated with skin color; those with little sin tend to have white skin, while more sinful folk have dark skin (Jacob 3:8, 9). When people come out of a state of unbelief and sin and repent, embracing the true religion and worshipping the true God, their skin subsequently turns from black to white (III Nephi 2:15). And to top it all off, when Jesus makes an appearance to ancient inhabitants of North America, he is white (III Nephi 19:30).

But there's more. In another holy book of the Mormon canon of revealed scripture, The Pearl of Great Price, additional racist beliefs and doctrines emerge. An elaborate racial-religious system is conveyed in which contemporary black people are understood as the direct descendants of two cursed Old Testament characters, Cain and Ham. As the descendants of such sinners (Cain murdered his brother, and Ham looked at his father naked), blacks are innately sinful by way of ancestry. Through their very genes they inherit the sinfulness of their ancestors and are thus an inferior people (Taggart 1970, 71). Apostle Orson Hyde deepened this religious notion of intrinsic black inferiority by declaring in 1845 that the subordinate status of black people was the result not only of blacks' genetic ties to Cain and Ham, but also of events that took place in a spiritual, premortal existence. According to Hyde, at some point in prehistory in some cosmic realm, God had fought a battle with Lucifer and certain premortal spirits hadn't taken a side in the battle but had remained passive during the fight. Because of their passivity, these premortal spirits were given black bodies as punishment once they became mortal here on earth (Bringhurst 1981, 87; Hansen 1981, 196).

Why did early Mormonism develop such a racist cosmology? Why did it create a worldview in which black skin was equated with an inner state of sinfulness? Why did it construct a religious philosophy in which black people were regarded as the descendants of cursed biblical characters, thereby justifying their inferior and subordinate status? The bottom line is that these ideas are simply not unique to Mormonism. These ideas were permeating American society in the early nineteenth century, when Mormonism was established (Hansen 1981). As Henry Bowden (1981, xi) has succinctly noted, "like all religious expressions, Mormonism reflected the historical conditions in which it arose and took distinctive shape. . . . [F]aithful Mormons embodied social attitudes common to the culture that nurtured them." Even the specific notion that blacks were the descendants of Cain and Ham was a common cultural-religious belief, especially among slaveholding Christians of the South (Smith 1972; Stanton 1951). Sure, Mormonism had its particular spin on race matters, but by and large we can best explain Mormon racist beliefs as simply an outgrowth or reflection of the general, widespread racism that permeated white Protestant America in the days when Mormonism was being developed.

That said, what these racist Mormon beliefs and doctrines led to in practice was an institutional exclusion of all black men from the Mormon priesthood (Bush and Mauss 1984). And it must be understood that unlike the Catholic priesthood—which is made up of a small, self-selecting group of religious virtuosos—in Mormonism *all* good-standing men over the age of twelve constitute the priesthood. It is in fact a lay priesthood, composed of all devout male members (women are excluded). Thus, by denying black men the right to enter the priesthood, the Mormon religion was effectively barring black men from full and equal membership in the religion. Without admittance to the priesthood, black men were denied important religious rights and privileges, such as the ability to partake in various ritual ceremonies in the most sacred rooms of the temple, including the "sealing" of marriage for eternity, which is necessary for full exaltation in the hereafter.

It was the second leader of the Mormon religion, Brigham Young,[3] who explained in 1849 that "because Cain cut off the lives [sic] of Abel . . . the Lord cursed Cain's seed and prohibited them the priesthood" (Bringhurst 1981, 84). This position would hold strong for over a century. One hundred years after Young's pronouncement, on August 17, 1949, the LDS First Presidency publicly declared:

> The attitude of the Church with reference to Negroes remains as it has always stood. It is not a matter of the declaration of a policy but of direct commandment from the Lord . . . to the effect that Negroes may become members of the Church but that they are not entitled to the priesthood at the present time. The prophets of the Lord have made several statements as to the operation of the principle. President Brigham Young said: "Why are so many of the inhabitants of the earth cursed with a skin of blackness? It comes in consequence of their fathers rejecting the power of the holy priesthood, and the law of God. They will go down to death. And when all the rest of the children have received their blessings in the holy priesthood, then that curse will be removed from the seed of Cain, and they will then come up and possess the priesthood, and received all the blessings which we are now entitled to."
>
> The position of the Church regarding the Negro may be understood when another doctrine of the church is kept in mind, namely, that the conduct of spirits in the premortal existence has some determining effect upon the conditions and circumstances under which these spirits take on mortality . . . under this principle there is no injustice whatsoever involved in this deprivation as to the holding of the priesthood by the Negroes. (Bringhurst 1981, 230)[4]

Twenty years later, in 1969, the LDS First Presidency again publicly reiterated its position:

[W]e believe the Negro, as well as those of other races, should have his full Constitutional privileges as a member of society, and we hope that members of the Church everywhere will do their part as citizens to see that these rights are held inviolate. Each citizen must have equal opportunities and protection under the law with reference to civil rights.

However, matters of faith, conscience, and theology are not within the purview of civil law . . .

From the beginning of this dispensation, Joseph Smith and all succeeding presidents of the Church have taught that Negroes, while spirit children of a common Father, and the progeny of our earthly parents Adam and Eve, were not yet to receive the priesthood, for reasons which we believe are known to God, but which He has not made fully known to man.

Our living prophet, President David O. McKay, has said, "The seeming discrimination by the Church toward the Negro is not something which originated with man; but goes back into the beginning with God . . ." (Bringhurst 1981, 231).

This pronouncement of 1969 is especially fascinating. Unlike its predecessor of twenty years, implicit in this 1969 proclamation is the notion that the Mormons themselves are uncomfortable with the denial of priesthood to black men—that they are in an admitted state of ignorance concerning its value or purpose—but that they are ultimately just following orders from the Lord, mysterious as those orders may be. They insist that the responsibility of the denial of black priesthood has nothing to do with them, but rests solely with the Lord. And it should be noted that this 1969 declaration of priesthood denial did not merely reflect the sentiments of those in power. A 1972 Louis Harris Poll found that 70 percent of all Mormons living in Utah opposed granting blacks the right to hold the priesthood. Additionally, one-third of those polled agreed that the 1960s swelling controversy over black priesthood denial was part of a "black conspiracy" to destroy the Mormon religion (Bringhurst 1981, 172).

But then, in 1978, something miraculous happened. Only six years after the Harris Poll just mentioned above, the Mormon hierarchy purportedly received a new order directly from God. This time, the LDS First Presidency publicly announced:

He [the Lord] has heard our prayers, and by revelation has confirmed that the long-promised day has come when every faithful, worthy man in the Church may receive the priesthood, with power to exercise its divine authority, and enjoy with his loved ones every blessing that flows therefrom, including the blessings of the temple. Accordingly, all worthy male members of the church may be ordained to the priesthood without regard for race or color. (Bringhurst 1981, 178)

What had happened? After over a hundred and fifty years of priesthood denial, the Church of Jesus Christ of Latter-day Saints officially welcomed black men fully into the fold. Had God really changed his mind concerning whether or not blacks could enter the Mormon priesthood? Or did the Mormon religion simply acclimate itself to a latter-twentieth-century United States wherein such overt racism was simply untenable?

According to the official Mormon version, here's what took place:

Spencer W. Kimball was the president of the church at the time—its institutional and spiritual leader. He recalled that, in the wake of growing public scrutiny and criticism of the priesthood denial policy,

I walked to the temple and ascended to the fourth floor where we have our solemn assemblies . . . After everybody had gone out of the temple, I knelt and prayed. I prayed with much fervency. I knew that something was before us that was extremely important to many of the children of God . . . Day after day I went alone and with great solemnity and seriousness in the upper rooms of the temple, and there I offered my soul and offered my efforts to go forward with the program (Kimball 1982, 450).

In addition to his solo prayers to God, Kimball raised the issue with others within the Mormon hierarchy. Several Mormon leaders began to earnestly discuss the issue with one another. And then they began praying together, entreating the Lord as a group. It was during one such group prayer session, led by Kimball, that the Lord's new will became apparent. As one of the men present recalled:

It was during this prayer that the revelation came. The Spirit of the Lord rested mightily upon us all; we felt something akin to what happened on the day of Pentecost and at the dedication of the Kirkland

Temple . . . we all heard the same voice, received the same message, and became personal witnesses that the word received was the mind and will and voice of the Lord (Embry 1994, 31).

Was it really the Spirit of the Lord that "rested mightily" upon those Mormon leaders immediately prior to the 1978 revelation ending black priesthood denial, or was it the spirit of a post–civil rights American society? There are several factors that lead me to suspect the latter as the better answer.

First, institutional racism in the United States came under direct attack with the civil rights movement, most popularly energized by Martin Luther King Jr. in the 1950s and '60s. In the ensuing years, the movement for racial equality won dramatic results: the desegregation of schools, an end to legal discrimination in public facilities, employment, and housing, and the passing of the 1965 Voting Rights Act, to name a few of the more prominent victories (Eitzen and Zinn 2001, 535). Though black Americans continued to suffer from a plethora of institutional racist realities (police brutality, denial of home-loan funding, limited business support, etc.), the United States was fundamentally changed by the civil rights movement—including Mormonism (Hansen 1981, 199). Racism—though not disappearing—could no longer be enforced legally, nor taken for granted culturally.

Second, the Mormon church began to directly feel the heat in the wake of the civil rights movement in a spate of specific actions (Embry 1994; Bringhurst 1981). Throughout the 1960s, the NAACP began to publicly decry Mormon racism, writing editorials in newspapers, filing legal charges against specific incidents of racist policies, boycotting various public facilities throughout Utah which were blatant in their discriminatory policies. Major universities began to boycott Brigham Young University, barring their sports teams from competing against the major Mormon university. Even when other universities would allow their sports teams to compete with Brigham Young University, the athletes themselves often refused to do so—as was the case with basketball players from San Jose State, football players from the University of Wyoming, and members of the University of Texas–El Paso track team. Whenever the Brigham Young sports teams went elsewhere to play, they were often greeted by picketing and harassment. Clergy throughout the United States began opposing visiting concerts of the Mormon Tabernacle Choir. And pressure mounted not only from the outside but from within as well; a handful of antiracist Mormons began pushing the issue within their own communities, publicly criticizing their leaders for their racist beliefs and policies (Taggart 1970).

And a third factor contributing to the end of Mormon priesthood denial was the dramatic growth of Mormonism abroad, specifically in racially diverse countries such as Nigeria and Brazil. Mormon conversions were in abundance in Brazil in the 1960s and 1970s, but with such a colorful mix of racial and ethnic identities in that country, it was quite difficult for Mormon officials to really tell who was white and who wasn't—therefore, priesthood denial couldn't be enforced with any real certainty! (Grover 1990). As Hansen (1981, 203) relates:

> It was quite obvious that some time before the official revelation of 1978, some Brazilians were ordained to the priesthood who had Negro ancestry. When the church announced in 1975 that a temple would be built in Sao Paulo, the die was in effect cast. For under the old policy neither males nor females with "Negro blood" could have been allowed into the temple. To have a large population of second class Saints in Brazil in the 1970s was clearly unthinkable.

Today there are still only a handful of black Mormons within the United States. But people of color around the world are embracing the new religion, especially in South America. And those nonwhite worthy males over the age of twelve are no longer denied the priesthood as a punishment for their "genetic" links to Cain and Ham. Instead, they are welcomed as full brothers in the faith, thanks to the new revelation in 1978.

What do you think? Did God really change his mind? Or did the antiracist winds of 1960s and 1970s America—and the changing demographics of the growing church abroad—simply make priesthood denial to black men egregiously anachronistic and culturally intolerable?

Now on to a second example illustrating the fact that social life unavoidably determines and influences religious life. Let's switch from race matters to gender matters and discuss how the sociocultural phenomenon of feminism has affected and informed contemporary religious life.

Let me start with a quick anecdote.

Last year, I went with some friends to a new vegetarian Chinese restaurant. The little establishment was tucked away in an ugly strip mall, among a dozen other ugly strip malls. Its interior was stark: twelve cold tables with plastic chairs, no plants, drab colors. But it did have an impressive variety of vegetarian food options. As I stood at the counter deciding what to order, I noticed hanging on the wall a few pictures of a Chinese woman. Beneath each portrait was the inscription: "The Supreme Master Ching Hai." I then noticed that beside the cash register was a stack of pamphlets and booklets with information about this woman and her spiritual teachings. It quickly dawned on me that this little eatery was not merely the only all-vegetarian Chinese restaurant in Upland, California—it was also a religious outpost, tied to a movement of followers who believe that this woman, Ching Hai, is a "supreme master," an enlightened individual with divine wisdom and sacred insights for all of humanity.[5]

I took a booklet with me as we were leaving. It had Master Ching Hai's picture on it and it was titled *The Key of Immediate Enlightenment*. Now here's what struck me. On the very first page, in a little shaded box, was the following blurb titled "A Little Message":

In speaking of God, or the Supreme Spirit, we will use original non-sexist terms to avoid the argument about whether God is a She or a He.

She + He = Hes (as in Mess)
Her + Him = Hirm (as in Firm)
Hers + His = Hiers (as in Beers)

Example: When God wants, Hes makes things happen according to Hiers will to suit Hirm.

I sat in my car and stared at that little shaded box and grinned a sociologist of religion's grin. There it was: feminism's unmistakable influence on contemporary religious life, as exhibited on page 1 of this little booklet found in a small vegetarian restaurant in a strip mall in southern California. Such a message in a religious text would be unthinkable one hundred years ago. Or even fifty years ago. And it would still be unthinkable in many parts of the world today. At no other time in human history—and in very few places on the planet—would such an explicit directive concerning "non-sexist" pronouns for God be conceivable, let alone publishable. But here and now, at the dawn of the twenty-first century, it is there. And it "makes sense" to the twenty-first-century American mind. That is, we can understand what it means in terms of religious and cultural significance, and we can understand why whoever wrote it felt compelled to do so. We may scoff at it for its hyper–"political correctness" or we may applaud it for its progressive attempts at establishing nonpatriarchal language for talking about the divine. But either way, what is important sociologically is that we recognize that its very existence is only possible because feminism has been such a significant player in American life—and elsewhere around the globe—for several decades now.

Feminism has been defined by bell hooks (1984, 24) as the "struggle to end sexist oppression." Laura Kramer (2001, 9) defines feminism as "the view that women are oppressed in significant ways and that this oppression should be ended." Eitzin and Zinn (2001, 328) refer to feminism as that which supports "women's equality." My own understanding of feminism is that it is an ideological and political movement based upon the recognition that women and men are equally human and should enjoy equal choices and options concerning how they want to live. Feminism is what won women the right to vote in 1920. It is the movement which has opened up to many women countless professions that had previously been closed. Feminism is largely to thank for the fact that my first daughter was delivered by a female doctor, that my female cousin is an assistant district attorney, that my wife is pursuing a career as a filmmaker, and that I feel good and comfortable about spending so much time raising my children, making them a higher priority in my life than my career. Feminism's impact on American life has indeed been quite remarkable, as Christel Manning (1999) specifically details:

> In 1995, more than half of all bachelors and masters degrees were awarded to women, compared to about 25 and 14 percent respectively in 1950 . . . about one-third of women now have managerial positions (up from one-fifth in 1970), and there are more women lawyers and doctors than ever before: women received 42.2 percent of law degrees

and 34 percent of medical degrees in 1990, compared to 2.5 and 5.5 percent respectively in 1960.

There isn't a single social institution—from the military to the family—which hasn't been engaged with the ideologies and demands of feminism. And religion is no exception. As Lester Kurtz (1995, 228) notes, "one of the most profound of modern movements—that affects all levels of society as well as all societies—is the demand for equality by women . . . and this movement, in its various forms, challenges the very roots of the major world religions." And as Jack Wertheimer (1993, 19) corroborates, feminism has "challenged all American religious groups by raising profound questions about both gender roles and sexual mores. Few organized religious groups have been able to ignore the feminist agenda."

Wherever feminism is a potent cultural force, religion will have to contend with it (Watling 2002; Gross 1996; Castelli 2001; Runzo and Martin 2000; Swatos 1994; Daly 1968; Manning 1999; Juschka 2001; Haddad and Findly 1985). Religion may fight against and resist feminism or it may incorporate and accept feminism, but either way, feminism will be an unavoidable part of religion's universe. I came face to face with this reality while studying the Jewish community of Eugene, Oregon.

When I moved to Eugene in 1989, there was only one synagogue, Temple Beth Israel. It was a humble, little, inauspicious, one-story building tucked away in a sleepy neighborhood on a quiet street. Since the 1950s, it alone served the Jewish community of Eugene as the sole congregation in town. And then, in the early 1990s, while I was midway through graduate school at the University of Oregon, things began to fall apart. The congregation experienced intense infighting and internal division, which led to an eventual schism. This secluded Jewish community that had always prided itself on its solidarity and unity suddenly found itself going through a painful divorce. And like all too many divorces, the division had been quite acrimonious. As one of the members involved in the schism succinctly recalled: "It was ugly" (Zuckerman 1999, 16).

What had happened? Why had this tiny Jewish community broken apart? What differences had surfaced that had been so irreconcilable?

Fascinated by this process of communal strife and congregational separation, I jumped into the fray and wrote my dissertation on the
schism of Eugene's Jewish community, engaging in over a year's worth
of participatory fieldwork and interviewing over fifty individuals
(Zuckerman 1997, 1999).

There were many reasons the congregation broke apart. There
were personal antagonisms that had festered for years; some people
just didn't like other people, for a variety of idiosyncratic reasons.
And the rabbi also played a role as a distinctly controversial figure; as
is the case in probably every congregation, he had his devoted fans
and his disgruntled critics. There were also many political differences
which divided the congregants, especially concerning Israel; some
people favored a hard military response against the Palestinian movement for independence, while others believed in pursuing a more
peaceful, conciliatory two-state solution. And there were differences
of opinion concerning a myriad of additional Jewish cultural/reli-
gious issues, such the acceptance of intermarried couples, adherence
to kosher dietary laws, the use of modern language and music during
worship services, rewriting of certain prayers such as the *Aleynu* to
make them less ethnocentric, and so on.

But the greatest source of tension, the one issue that most dramatically and explicitly divided the congregation above all else—the one
underlying controversy that every single one of my informants described as being central to the schism—was the struggle over matters
of gender. Irreconcilable differences concerning the roles and rights
of men and women in the synagogue were ultimately at the heart of
the split (Zuckerman 1997).

Traditional/Orthodox Judaism is decidedly patriarchal, as Susan
Sered (1992, 15) explains:

> Traditional Judaism addresses the deity in the masculine gender,
> teaches that God's message was conveyed primarily through men
> (Abraham, Moses), bestows the privilege of leadership (rabbinate and
> priesthood) upon men, has traditionally excluded women from such
> central areas of religious expression as study and vocal participation in
> the synagogue, places prohibitions upon menstruating and postpartum

women, and discriminates against women in matters of inheritance.
Men write the prayers and make the laws . . .

   Women are systematically barred from access to Jewish knowledge . . .

Though Temple Beth Israel was never as fully Orthodox as described
above, it was founded as a Conservative synagogue which leaned more
toward traditionally patriarchal forms of organization and worship. But
with the death of the community's first rabbi in the mid-1970s and the
subsequent hiring of a new one, Temple Beth Israel started to change.
Institutional and religious modifications and alterations were steadily
enacted throughout the 1980s, changes which were often spearheaded
by the new rabbi's feminist wife and which were often related to gender.

   First came the inclusion of women in every aspect of synagogue rituals. Women were allowed and encouraged to publicly read from the
Torah, to lead prayers, to speak, to sing—in short, to engage in every aspect of religious activity that in traditional Judaism are reserved for men
only. Then came the changing of the wording of certain prayers to make
them more gender inclusive. Many Hebrew prayers which are recited
weekly (and sometimes daily) can be considered by some to be either
exclusionary of women or inherently sexist in that God is referred to in
specifically male terms. Many men and women of Temple Beth Israel
successfully lobbied to have such prayers revised to fit their feminist-
informed sensibilities. So, for example, one of Judaism's central prayers
is the *Ameedah*, which affirms God's power and loving kindness. This
prayer also includes a mention of Judaism's patriarchs:

> *You abound in blessings . . . Adonai our God. God of our fathers. God of*
> *Abraham, God of Isaac, God of Jabob . . .*

This traditional version of the *Ameedah* was changed at Temple
Beth Israel to be more gender inclusive:

> *You abound in blessings. Adonai or God. God of our fathers and mothers. God*
> *of Abraham and Sarah. God of Isaac and Rebecca. God of Jacob, and Rachel*
> *and Leah . . .*

Eventually, by the early 1990s, every single prayer had been rewrit-
ten so that matriarchs as well as patriarchs were listed, all references to

sons would also include daughters, and God was always referred to in gender-neutral terms (from "Father" to "Parent" or from "Lord" to "Guardian" and so forth).

Most people welcomed and appreciated these feminist-inspired changes. But some did not. A few members of the synagogue began to resent these gender-conscious changes in prayer and practice.

As one male member explained:

> And then they changed the liturgy to be sexually neutral. Where when one speaks of the creator of the universe he uses the word "He,"—doesn't mean that it's a man, a masculine person. It's just a way of speaking. So they did a lot of crazy things. Which for a while, you know, were tolerable. But then it got to a point where it was just beyond the point of no return (Zuckerman 1999, 123).

As another male member commented:

> [The rabbi] is so left-wing . . . anything traditional—out the window. And he was pushing the *shule* [synagogue] all the way to the left and basically, you know, had a very . . . feminist agenda . . . Well, partly because his wife is such a, you know . . . a very extreme feminist. Which, I mean—none of us had any problems with that at all—it just basically, it took the *shule* from being a middle-of-the-road, welcoming place for everybody, to a very, very extreme left-wing agenda, and people didn't want to be part of it anymore (Zuckerman 1999, 122).

From a female member:

> I found it arrogant and repugnant to tinker around with prayers that were—depending on what prayer it was, it may have been a prayer that was a thousand years old or two thousand years old—to tinker with a prayer or custom because it didn't seem politically correct in 1990 or 1995, it just seemed the height of intellectual arrogance (Zuckerman 1999, 126).

And another female member:

> They were very big on gender issues. So, you know, you could never say "He" for God . . . It seemed like the more Jewish I was getting, the less Jewish they were getting. It was really bizarre . . . To me it got embarrassing because they would start off services and they would say, "Okay,

we're gonna go by the prayer book except any time you see this word, substitute this word" . . . and . . . I said, "But you know, the Hebrew word is masculine" . . . you know, I just thought it was kind of stupid . . . It seemed to be more concerned with political correctness than it did with traditional Judaism (Zuckerman 1997, 361).

This small group of people within the congregation who did not like the many changes that were enacted throughout the 1980s and early 1990s began to consider their options. Somebody suggested that they simply cease to partake in the watered-down, feminist-inspired Judaism now reigning at their synagogue and try getting back to a more traditional form of Jewish worship. This suggestion caught their imaginations, and many from this group—both men and women—suddenly felt inspired to start living and practicing their Judaism in a more traditional, conservative manner. And they subsequently began meeting in a backroom of the synagogue for weekly prayer services, rather than worship in the main sanctuary with the rest of the congregation.

The situation seemed perfect: those who preferred the more modern, gender-neutral approach could attend services in the main sanctuary, and those who were interested in a more traditional approach could attend services in the back room. But the solution was short-lived. Everything fell apart when those in the main sanctuary became aware of the fact that those in the back room had erected a *mehitzah*. A *mehitzah* is a physical divider or barrier—usually some sort of small wall or humble fence made of thin wood—that is customarily placed between men and women during traditional Orthodox worship services.

As one man recalled:

At one point the people in the [traditional] group decided they couldn't abide by the liberalism in the regular service. They wanted to have services in the back of the synagogue . . . and then they decided that that wasn't traditional enough, and they had to put up a *mehitzah*. And then the firestorm (Zuckerman 1999, 165).

As another man explained:

I think the issue that actually caused the split was the separation of men and women—the *mehitzah*. The Orthodox group wanted women separated and wanted a division. And a very significant membership said, "That is morally repugnant to me . . . we cannot allow a division of men and women in prayer in our synagogue." And I think that's the issue that actually sent one group packing (Zuckerman 1999, 166).

The underlying idea behind physically separating men and women during such services is that by having the sexes separate, each can focus their attention on prayer and God, rather than on one another. The *mehitzah* is also a physical symbol recognizing men and women's innate spiritual differences. As one of my male informants explained:

Men and women have been separated in religious practices going back to the times of the Temple, the Second Temple . . . Judaism acknowledges that just like there are physical differences between men and women . . . there are psychological differences between men and women . . . there are spiritual differences between men and women . . . Judaism acknowledges the differences and is constructed differently for men and women (Zuckerman 1999, 211).

Of course, not everyone agreed with such sentiments. A female informant said:

The purpose of the *mehitzah* is to divide people. To exclude a group of people. And that's what it does . . . it's apartheid. It's the back of the bus. You know, women don't count in the *minyan*.[6] And your voice is despicable, and you're not a full human being (Zuckerman 1999, 188).

The battle over this *mehitzah* became the single most divisive issue the congregation had ever faced. And it was an issue laden with heavy symbolic weight, which is often the case in religious disputes (Sered 1997; Kniss 1996). For members of the newly Orthodox group, the *mehitzah* was a symbol of Jewish tradition, as well as an appropriate recognition and enforcement of the physical, psychological, and spiritual differences between men and women. For members in the feminist camp, the *mehiztah* was a symbol of patriarchal oppression and suspicious religious fundamentalism.

Those in the traditional camp felt it was their right to worship in the back room as they saw fit, *mehitzah* included. But the more feminist-minded members of the synagogue, those who worshipped in the main sanctuary, were horrified that a *mehitzah* would be put up anywhere on synagogue premises, back rooms included.

As one woman explained:

> The ultrafeminists at Temple Beth Israel became very alarmed— including the rabbi's wife—that there was a *mehitzah* anywhere on Temple Beth Israel's property . . . They saw it as an offense to God and to, you know, politically correct Jews and it couldn't be allowed (Zuckerman 1999, 167).

As the rabbi's wife explained:

> This synagogue was always democratic. This synagogue never had inequality. So all of a sudden, what you're doing by having a *mehitzah* is inviting inequality into equality. And I know I have to be a tolerant human being, but . . . I will not tolerate intolerance (Zuckerman 1999, 169).

Eventually, the feminist camp circulated a petition declaring that if the traditional group in the back room would not take down their *mehitzah* dividing men and women, they would have to leave. And of course, it was the latter scenario that occurred. The small Orthodox group left Temple Beth Israel, rented a worship space, hired themselves their own rabbi, and suddenly where there had been only one synagogue for decades, now there are two.

Temple Beth Israel's fight over the *mehitzah* was not unique. Many similar struggles and splits over this very issue have occurred in Jewish congregations throughout the United States (Joseph 1992; Plaskow 1990). And Jewish communities are not the only ones wrestling with differences and challenges concerning gender regulation. Gender-related debates and difficulties have occurred—and continue to occur—within Catholicism (Iadarola 1985; Wallace 1993; Manning 1999), Episcopalianism (Perlinger 1992), Protestant Christianity (Brasher 1998; Balmer 1994; Brown 1994; Beaman 1999), Eastern Orthodoxy (Manolache 1990), Buddhism (Cabezon 1992), Islam (Hoodfar 1997; Haddad and Esposito 1998; Riesebrodt 1993; Moaddel 1998), Mormonism (Bennion 1998), Seventh-Day Adventists (Dudley 1996), New Religious Movements (Goldman 1999; Aidala 1985; Jacobs 1989, 1991), Spiritualist groups (Haywood

1983), and a plethora of additional Protestant denominations, particularly concerning the issue of female ordination (Chaves 1997).

This chapter had one goal: to illustrate the notion that social trends can and inevitably do influence religious life. I picked two examples: changes in our society affecting racism and its reflection in Mormon doctrine and practice, and the impact of feminism on a small Jewish community in Eugene, Oregon. In the next chapter, I will look at the process going in the other direction—how religious forces can influence and affect other aspects of social life.

Notes

1. However, thousands of Mormons do still practice polygamy—polygyny specifically (Bennion 1998). These Mormons are considered apostates by the church in Salt Lake City. But it is important to remember that they consider themselves the *true* Mormons, and the church in Salt Lake City the heretical branch!
2. For faithful believers the Book of Mormon is a direct revelation from God that Joseph Smith miraculously translated in the 1820s from golden plates, which subsequently disappeared after his translation was complete. For skeptical nonbelievers, it is a book which Joseph Smith wrote himself, using various sources available to him at the time, as well as his imagination (Persuitte 2000).
3. According to Brigham Young, race mixing was a sin in the eyes of God, eternally punishable by death (quoted in Hansen 1981, 195).
4. Please note that the full declarations from 1949, 1969, and 1978 are substantially longer in their entirety; I am quoting selectively.
5. For more information on the Supreme Master Ching Hai, check out www.Godsdirectcontact.org.tw or www.Godsimmediatecontact.net.
6. A minyan is a quorum of ten men required to be present in order to read publicly from the Torah; in traditional Judaism, women cannot count toward the makeup of a minyan.

6

RELIGION AFFECTING
SOCIAL LIFE

I began the previous chapter with a discussion of W. E. B. Du Bois's classic *The Souls of Black Folk*. I homed in on chapter 12 from that book, "Of Alexander Crummell," discussing the racism young Crummell experienced as a black Christian in nineteenth-century America. I did so as a way to illustrate the notion that religion is always affected by the sociocultural environment within which it dwells. Because racism was so rampant and pervasive in nineteenth-century America, it was inevitable that the major religion of the country—Christianity—would echo, reflect, and at times even reinforce that racism.

But it is important to remember that racism did not defeat Alexander Crummell, nor did it destroy his faith. Despite the prejudice and discrimination he experienced as expressed by certain Christians, Crummell did not give up on Christianity. Just the opposite: he lived his life dedicated to God, faith, and charity. He spent years as a Christian missionary in Africa, he established Saint Luke's Episcopal Church in Washington, D.C., and he was a founder of the American Negro Academy. His life was devoted to battling racism and helping out his brothers and sisters, and these noble pursuits were rooted in his religious orientation.

Though Du Bois noted the degree to which racism pervaded American Christianity, both at the institutional and doctrinal level, he also acknowledged that Christianity was simultaneously a major source of comfort and strength in the life of African Americans (Zuckerman 2000). In chapter 10 of *The Souls of Black Folk*, "Of the

Faith of the Fathers," he spoke of the black church as "the social cen-
tre of Negro life in the United States." He went on to positively characterize the black church as

> the central club-house of a community . . . Various organizations meet
> here,—the church proper, the Sunday-school, two or three insurance
> societies, women's societies, secret societies, and mass meetings of vari-
> ous kinds. Entertainments, suppers, and lectures are held beside the five
> or six regular weekly religious services. Considerable sums of money are
> collected and expended here, employment is found for the idle,
> strangers are introduced, news is disseminated and charity distributed.
> At the same time this social, intellectual, and economic centre is a reli-
> gious centre of great power. Depravity, Sin, Redemption, Heaven, Hell,
> and Damnation are preached twice a Sunday . . . and few indeed of the
> community have the hardihood to withstand conversion. Back of this
> more formal religion, the Church often stands as a real conserver of
> morals, a strengthener of family life, and the final authority on what is
> Good and Right (Du Bois, 1989 [1903], 136).

The point is that religion—either in the life of one individual (i.e.,
Alexander Crummell) or in the workings of an entire community—
can be the very thing shaping, determining, and influencing lived social experience. Christianity shaped and formed Crummell's life and
aspirations, and Christianity—to a very large degree—has shaped
and formed much of African American life in general (Raboteau
1999). This brings me to the central theoretical argument of this
chapter: *just as the sociocultural environment influences religion, so too
does religion influence the sociocultural environment.* Religion can often
be a forceful determinant of social phenomena, shaping institutions,
affecting values, and influencing relationships. Religion plays a decisive role in informing gender norms, constructing sexuality, influencing political debates, spurring or hindering economic phenomena,
affecting racial matters, and contributing to ecological circumstances,
media forces, family structures, technological developments, artistic
movements, and so on.

It is a dialectical relationship: nonreligious elements of the sociocultural environment inevitably affect religious life, and religion per-

petually acts back upon and helps shape elements of the sociocultural environment. In the previous chapter I discussed the former side of the relationship. In this chapter, I will illustrate the latter side. To demonstrate how religion can be a determining, influential factor in constructing society/culture, I'll use two examples: (1) religion's influential role in the civil rights movement and (2) religion's influential role in our sex lives.

The civil rights movement was the sociopolitical struggle that took place in the United States in the 1950s and 1960s wherein African Americans successfully challenged and overturned various racist laws and practices. The civil rights movement represents one of the greatest social achievements in American history: people risking life and limb in the name of freedom, liberty, and democracy. The civil rights movement illustrates the ability of an underprivileged, victimized minority to successfully (and nonviolently) resist a government-supported, police-enforced, and majority-sustained unjust status quo. The civil rights movement serves as an example of what is possible when people unite in the name of human dignity. And it was a movement undeniably indebted to, and embedded in, religion (Billingsley 1998; Frederick 1999; Marsh 1999). The civil rights struggle drew deeply from black Christian ethics and ideals. Indeed, Christianity's presence within and impact upon the civil rights movement was so pervasive and profound that it provides a glaring example of the powerful causal influence religion can have in affecting, directing, and shaping the social world.

That a deep black Christian faith in God was the blood that flowed through the veins of the civil rights movement, informing and sustaining its members throughout the struggle, is evident in the many writings and speeches of the movement's undisputed leader, the Reverend Dr. Martin Luther King Jr.:

> Throughout this struggle for racial justice I have constantly asked God to remove all bitterness from my heart and to give me strength and courage . . . this constant prayer life and feeling of dependence on God have given me the feeling that I have divine companionship in the struggle. I know no other way to explain it. (King 1998, 118)

For King, reliance upon God was at the heart of his activism and optimism:

> If you do not have a deep and patient faith in God, you will be power-less to face the delays, disappointments, and vicissitudes that inevitably come. Without God, all our efforts turn to ashes . . . (King 1963, 75).

He preached to his dedicated followers that

> God does not forget his children who are the victims of evil forces. He gives us the interior resources to bear the burdens and tribulations of life. When we are in the darkness of some oppressive Egypt, God is a light unto our path . . . when the lamp of hope flickers and the candle of faith runs low, he restoreth our souls, giving us renewed vigor to carry on. He is with us not only in the noontime of fulfillment, but also in the midnight of despair. (King 1963, 65)

The burdens and tribulations that permeated the days and nights of black Americans prior to and during the civil rights movement were many (Levy 1998). After centuries of legal slavery, widespread rape, systematic destruction of the family unit, and the pervasive threat of deadly violence at any time, blacks in the South in the 1940s and 1950s found themselves living in a severely segregated, harshly hateful apartheid world wherein whites had established "a comprehensive system of domination" (Morris 1984, 1). Whites con-trolled all aspects of the government and economy. The police were entirely white, as were all judges and prosecutors. Blacks were essen-tially barred from participating in elections. Blacks were barred from living in designated "white" neighborhoods. Blacks were barred from most beaches, recreational facilities, theaters, and amusement parks. Blacks weren't allowed to eat in many restaurants, and if they were, they were restricted to designated sections. Blacks weren't allowed to stay in most hotels. Blacks were barred from all major colleges and universities, by law. Libraries and cemeteries were strictly segregated.

The pre–civil rights South was a world in which white ambulance drivers would abandon injured and dying people if they happened to be black; and even if the injured black people could get themselves to a hospital, the hospital would often refuse to admit them. It was a world wherein blacks who dared to challenge even the smallest aspect of segregated life found themselves fired, evicted, or arrested on vague/false charges, and once in police custody, often beaten or killed. It was a world in which perceived misbehavior on the part of a black child could lead to his murder; in 1955, Emmett Till, a fourteen-year-old black boy allegedly said "bye baby" to a white female drugstore clerk and was subsequently murdered by the clerk's husband and his brother. Though they boasted about the killing, both men were acquitted of any wrongdoing by an all-white jury. The South in the pre–civil rights period was a world wherein blacks who had fought for the United States overseas—in the name of democracy and liberty—came home to a country which denied them both; when Medgar Evers led a group of black veterans who had recently returned from fighting in World War II to the courthouse in his hometown of Decatur, Mississippi, with the intention of registering to vote, a white mob halted their movement, threatening to kill them if they proceeded. In some instances, the black veterans were actually murdered by their white countrymen: Isaac Woodward had spent over a year in the Philippines fighting the Japanese only to be killed by a white policeman two weeks after his return home to Aiken, South Carolina. Like the murderers of Emmett Till, the police officer who killed Woodward was acquitted of all charges. Such acquittals were routine; the South at that time was a world in which nearly all white murderers of blacks were systematically acquitted by all-white juries of any wrongdoing. It was a world wherein black homes and churches were periodically bombed—even when inhabited by men, women, and children: four little girls were killed when a bomb blew up the Sixteenth Street Baptist Church in Birmingham, Alabama, on September 15, 1963.

In short, the world the civil rights movement sought to change was one plagued by drastic social inequality in terms of poverty rates, educational opportunities, electoral representation, and legal protection—and it was also a world haunted by the constant threat and reality of violence. The civil rights movement bravely confronted this world and managed to soften and remove much of its visible ugliness and legalized horror.

While many social injustices and systemic inequalities related to race still plague the American South, much has changed for the better. The civil rights movement successfully brought about enormous and widespread social improvement (Fredrickson 1995, 263–264; Levy 1998, 125), achieving virtually all of its goals: the desegregation of public facilities, black enfranchisement, a dramatic reduction of the day-to-day humiliations of racist Jim Crow culture, the governmental banning of discrimination in employment and education, and improved protection from white violence and lynch mobs. Through marches, boycotts, sit-ins, demonstrations, and a variety of other nonviolent means, the participants of the civil rights movement made this country a safer, fairer, freer, and more democratic society.

As I have stated above, the civil rights movement cannot be understood without recognition of its predominantly black Christian character. Religiosity pervaded the movement in the following ways: (1) its leaders were largely religious, (2) its organization and mobilization efforts were made possible as a result of preexisting religious communal ties and establishments, and (3) its overarching ideology and spiritual underpinnings were explicitly Christian.

Of course, not all black leaders who fought for civil rights were religious; in fact some were actually quite antireligious (e.g., W. E. B. Du Bois and A. Philip Randolph). And not all black religious leaders were actively supportive of the struggle for civil rights (Thompson 1963, 35; Brink and Harris 1963, 108). But without question, the majority of the black leaders who did carry out the civil rights movement were faithful Christians (Billingsley 1998; Morris 1984). The most well known include the following clergymen: Martin Luther King Jr., Ralph Abernathy, Leon Sullivan, A. L. Davis, Samuel Williams, Kelly Miller Smith, T. J. Jemison, Daniel Speed, Glenn Smiley, Andrew Young, James Lawson, Ralph Mark Gilbert, Joseph Lowery, C. T. Vivian, Wyatt Walker, and Fred Shuttlesworth. Boycotts of segregated public buses—in Montgomery, Alabama, Baton Rouge, Louisiana, and Tallahassee, Florida—were the dramatic early conflicts of the civil rights movement, and these successful struggles were led almost entirely by ministers, as Fairclough (1987, 13) describes:

> The bus boycotts in Baton Rouge, Montgomery, and Tallahassee were
> led by ministers and organized through the black church. The Tallahas-
> see boycott movement, the Inter-Civic Council, numbered six clergymen

among its nine officers and was led by the Reverend C. K. Steele. The boycott organization in Montgomery, the Montgomery Improvement Association, was similarly top-heavy with men of the cloth, with two dozen ministers helping Martin Luther King keep the protest in motion. When the state of Alabama outlawed the National Association for the Advancement of Colored People, a clergyman, Fred Shuttlesworth, organized an alternative organization in Birmingham. Preachers were indeed moving into the vanguard of black protest in the South.

Christian leadership of the civil rights movement is evident when considering the hundreds of ministers who made up the Southern Christian Leadership Conference (SCLC). Founded in 1957, the SCLC was a confederation of black leaders and church organizations with branches throughout the South whose purpose was the acquisition of social justice for blacks employing nonviolent means. Christian ethics of peace and love were central tenets of the organization, and two-thirds of SCLC's board members were ministers (Fairclough 1987, 34). The founding SCLC board had thirty-six formal leadership positions; thirty-two of those positions were held by clergymen (Morris 1984, 87). While the National Association for the Advancement of Colored People (NAACP) achieved many legal victories, including the 1954 antisegregation judicial decision in *Brown v. Board of Education*, and while the Congress of Racial Equality (CORE) and the Student Nonviolent Coordinating Committee (SNCC) made headway in voter registration and desegregating public transportation and restaurants, the most substantial victories of the civil rights movement were made concrete in the Civil Rights Act of 1964 and Voting Rights Act of 1965, both coming as a direct result of the efforts of the SCLC (Fairclough 1987, 2). According to the black activist Bayard Rustin (1963, 38–39), the SCLC was the "sustaining mechanism" and "dynamic center" of the civil rights movement. According to Aldon Morris (1984, 77), "the Southern Christian Leadership Conference was the force that developed the infrastructure of the civil rights movement."

The Christian identity of Martin Luther King Jr.—the leader and visionary of the civil rights movement—deserves special emphasis. As a result of his public charisma, his commitment to nonviolence, his eloquence of written and oral expression, and the enormous personal sacrifices he endured, Martin Luther King personified the struggle for racial justice more than any one particular individual. Though he did not create or sustain the movement single-handedly—the hundreds of thousands of people who marched, protested, and were beaten and jailed *were* the movement—his leadership provided a unique guiding light for the struggle. Without his personal vision, political decision making, and individual touch, the movement would have been quite different in style and development. And Lewis Baldwin (1991) has convincingly argued that King's identity cannot be adequately understood without a firm grasp of his distinctly Christian background and orientation. King—a third-generation preacher, nourished in a distinctly black Christian tradition—was driven by what Baldwin (1991, 5) labels a "Christian Optimism," which was rooted in a cultural heritage stemming back to his slave forebears, affirming "that in spite of human suffering and the tragic circumstances of life, God will ultimately emerge triumphant over evil and bring liberation and salvation to all people."

King (1998, 77) himself described the importance of religion in his life, stating unambiguously that a direct connection with God laid the foundation for his courageous social activism:

> One night toward the end of January [1956] I settled into bed late, after a strenuous day . . . just as I was about to doze off the telephone rang. An angry voice said, "Listen, nigger, we've taken all we want from you; before next week you'll be sorry you ever came to Montgomery." I hung up, but I couldn't sleep . . .
>
> I got out of bed and began to walk the floor . . . I went to the kitchen and heated a pot of coffee. I was ready to give up . . .
>
> With my head in my hands, I bowed over the kitchen table and prayed . . .
>
> It seemed as though I could hear the quiet assurance of an inner voice saying: "Martin Luther, stand up for righteousness, Stand up for justice. Stand up for truth. And lo, I will be with you. Even until the end of the world" . . . at that moment I experienced the presence of the Divine as I had never experienced Him before. Almost at once my fears began to go. My uncertainty disappeared. I was ready to face anything.

King was not the only leader inspired by a relationship with his God. A comprehensive study of organizations and movements in the struggle for civil rights reveals an extended list of ministers at the helm of a variety of organizations in every state of the South (Davis 1998; Morris 1984; see also McAdam 1988).

There are significant sociological reasons why the leadership of the civil rights movement predominantly comprises ministers. To fight against racism in the South was to invite retaliation—often the loss of one's job. The overwhelming majority of blacks prior to and during the civil rights movement lived in poverty, employed as semi- or low-skilled laborers (Morris 1984, 1; Levy 1998, 125). As such, most simply could not afford the risk of unemployment. Preachers, however, were in the unique position of having employment safe from white retaliation. Thus, with a relatively high degree of economic independence, black ministers could get involved in the struggle without the same fear of loss of livelihood which threatened the majority of their black brethren (Fairclough 1987, 14; McAdam 1982, 135). However, to explain the role of Christian leadership in the civil rights movement as strictly a function of mere economics is missing a large part of the picture. After all, economic retaliation was often the least of these leaders' worries; the threat of being arrested, or shot, or of having one's relatives arrested or shot, or one's house or church bombed or burned was a persistent reality. The ministers who led the civil rights movement despite these violent threats did so out of a deep conviction that they were doing the Lord's will. The bottom line is that the civil rights movement was led by a group of strong and courageous leaders, leaders who were supported, guided, and assured by a distinctly Christian conviction.

Christianity was not only a hallmark of the leadership of the civil rights movement, but Christian communal ties were an essential ingredient of the movement and a key component of its success. The organization and mobilization of tens of thousands of people, which the civil rights movement required, were made possible by the existence of that single most important institution in black life: the church. According to Adam Fairclough (1987, 17), "as an organizational tool it was second to none." Since the times of slavery, the black church had always been the one place where blacks could maintain a relative degree of autonomy and agency (Du Bois 2003 [1903]; Raboteau 1999). In the 1950s and '60s, the black church provided community centers where meetings could be held, information could be disseminated, leaders could inspire the masses, and social networking was ensured. Black churches provided funds, staff, lodging, food, and refuge throughout the struggle; it was in the black churches that alternative means of transportation were arranged during bus boycotts, it was where youth meetings were held along with classes on nonviolence and voter registration, as well as prayer vigils and memorial services for murdered activists (Morris 1984; Fairclough 1987; Baldwin 1991; McAdam 1982). "The role of the Negro church in the present struggle," noted Martin Luther King, "is a unique sociological phenomenon peculiar to the Negro community of the South." It is, in short, "the headquarters of the Negro's struggle for full citizenship" (Baldwin 1991, 224–225).

The leaders of the civil rights movement were Christian, the headquarters of the movement were churches, and permeating the entire struggle was a black Christian idealism (Moses 1993; Raines 1977, 69). Bible readings, prayers, and gospel songs perpetually infused the movement and sustained the activists. The cornerstone of the movement was a Christian ethic of nonviolence, predicated on love for those who hate. As Aldon Morris (1984, 62) explains:

> The religious doctrines of the black church provided the ideological framework through which the doctrine of nonviolence was disseminated . . . For years blacks had been taught that Christian love conquered hate and that the individual should love everyone, including oppressors.

The civil rights movement was thus not merely about gaining social equality between the races. It was also about raising humanity to a higher ethical and spiritual plane. King's insistence upon nonviolence was politically astute, to be sure, but it also served as an illustration for all the world to see of the ability and power of the oppressed to "turn the other cheek" in the face of police dogs, batons, and fire hoses (Goldberg 1991, 145). In other words, the civil rights movement was more than a political crusade—it was also a religious crusade. As Albert Raboteau (1999, 113) clearly describes it:

> King argued that blacks had to use nonviolent methods to achieve their goals, not only because violence had no chance of success, but because nonviolence was the morally superior way to act. Nonviolence was not

simply a political tactic, it was a way of life, the perfect method for translating Christian love into social action . . . Nonviolence was based upon the firm conviction that suffering was redemptive because it could transform both the sufferer and the oppressor; it tried to convert, not to defeat, the opponent . . .

For King, and those who followed his leadership, the goal of the civil rights movement was to "save the soul of the nation."

In sum, the civil rights movement profoundly changed the United States, and it was a movement deeply Christian in nature. I have provided this brief historical discussion of the movement because, as Emerson and Smith (2000, 45) have rightly concluded, it offers a clear sociohistorical example of "the power of religion to call for and realize change."

Now on to a second example of how religion can be a significant factor in influencing lived social experience: religion's impact on our sex lives.

The relationship between religion and sex has long fascinated me, and I remember the very day my fascination began: it was on a rainy Saturday morning in Eugene, Oregon, in March 1992. I was an undergraduate at the local university, living in a filthy and wonderful blue house on High Street with several other students. On this particular Saturday morning, one of my housemates, Heather, came into my room and plopped herself down on my bed, mildly distraught. She had just come home, having spent the night at her boyfriend's apartment. There she sat, slumped on the edge of my bed, with her head in her hands.

"What's wrong?" I asked.

"Oh, I just feel so terrible . . ." she replied.

"What happened?"

"Dil and I had sex last night."

She sighed deeply, and left it at that. We sat there quietly for a few moments. I pondered her response, and soon found myself feeling slightly perplexed. So they had sex . . . *and*? There must be something more to explain her despair. Heather and Dil had been dating for several months, and I knew that they had been sexually active for quite a while. But there Heather sat on my bed as though something was sadly wrong. I became concerned, and suddenly began thinking of all the bad things that can go along with sex.

"Did . . . did . . . something happen," I asked. "I mean . . . .did he . . . ?"

"No, we just had sex."

"Did you want to?"

"Yes."

"Did he want to?"

"Yes."

"Were you really drunk or wasted or something?"

"No."

"Was there some kind of abuse or violence?"

"No."

"Did you not use protection?"

"We used protection."

"So what's wrong then?"

She lifted her head out of her hands and replied frankly, "We just had sex, that's all. I always feel terribly guilty after having sex—*don't you?*"

Guilty after consensual, mutually satisfying sex? *Huh?* I told Heather that I had never felt guilty after sex. In fact, I always felt quite the opposite the following morning: like the world was a grand and joyful place.

Thus began a two-hour conversation; I wanted to know why sex produced feelings of guilt and subsequent depression in Heather, and she wanted to know why it didn't produce such feelings in me. At some point in this lengthy discussion, Heather came to the conclusion that her feelings after sex must be directly tied to her having been raised a Catholic. And I figured that my lack of guilt around sex must be related to the fact that I was raised in an irreligious home (we were Jewish, but strictly in the cultural-ethnic sense). Our speculations concerning our guilt feelings around sex—or lack thereof—as being related to our religious identities were confirmed years later, when I came upon some research dealing with this very matter. What I found was that scholarly research has demonstrated a notable relationship between religion and sex guilt (Wyatt and Dunn 1991; Gil 1990; Weis 1983; Peterson 1964), especially among college students (Daugherty and Burger, 1984).

Religion is an undeniably influential factor in how many of us feel about sex, how we engage in sex, how often, and with whom (Manning and Zuckerman 2004; Parrinder 1996). And even people who aren't personally religious are still susceptible to absorbing and internalizing (to varying degrees) the religious currents of their culture, particularly when it comes to issues of sex and sexuality. One of the pioneering empirical researchers of human sexuality, Alfred Kinsey, observed over half a century ago that "there is nothing in the English-American social structure which has had more influence upon present patterns of sexual behavior than the religious grounds of that culture" (Kinsey 1948, 465). It is simply impossible to understand human sexuality without paying proper attention to the religious beliefs and practices of the cultural context within which sex and sexuality play themselves out (Delameter 1989; Tannahill 1980; Denison 1998).

Of course, there is no one single religious approach to sex. As Bryan S. Turner (1991, 112) notes, "religious orientations to human sexuality have occupied a variety of positions along a continuum between total denial and orgy." Every religious tradition has its own particular values, norms, teachings, and orientations to sex and sexuality. And furthermore, every distinct religious tradition is itself characterized by internal division and debate; within any one particular religious tradition there always exist diverse, competing, and contradictory approaches to sex and sexuality.

For example, consider the Shakers and the Oneida Perfectionists (Foster 1984). These were two relatively small religious groups located in the northeastern United States which were at their most successful peaks in the early-mid-1800s. Both considered themselves devoutly Christian, and yet they constructed completely opposite approaches to sex. The Shakers considered all sex as sinful; perpetual celibacy for all adherents was required. In direct contrast, the Oneida Perfectionists believed that sex was potentially holy, and communal ("complex") sexual relations among all adult adherents were required. Both groups found inspiration and justification for their dramatically opposing approaches to sex within the same Bible, and both believed their particular orientation to human sexuality was moral—the very will of God.

For a contemporary example of how even under the rubric of the same religion we can find dramatically different orientations to sex, consider the Shiloh Youth Revival Movement and The Family/Children of God. Again, both Christian. Both countercultural, communal movements that reached popular peaks among young North Americans throughout the late 1960s and 1970s. For the Shiloh movement, human sexuality was understood as existing in direct conflict with spiritual pursuits. Premarital, extramarital, and homosexual sex were all viewed as major sins, and even sex within marriage—though permitted—was merely tolerated (Isaacson 1995; Stewart, Richardson, and Simmonds 1976). In contrast, among The Family/Children of God, extramarital sex was viewed as a positive way to spread God's love (Bainbridge 1997). Women within the movement were expected to have sex with as many men as possible in the wider public as a way to bring them to Jesus, and this "flirty fishing" was to be accepted and encouraged by their husbands (Williams 1998).

The Family/Children of God, the Shakers, the Shiloh Youth Revival Movement, and the Oneida Perfectionists provide glaring, explicit examples of just how diverse religious approaches to sex can be, even within the same nominal faith, in this case, Christianity. And diversity in values, beliefs, and norms concerning sex gets even more apparent when we look at distinctly different religions over time and from different parts of the world (Parrinder 1996; Jung, Hunt, and Balakrishnan 2001; Manning and Zuckerman 2004). From Buddhist sexual renunciation (Sponberg 2004) to Jewish rabbinical lauding of the female orgasm (Biale 1992), from Catholic priesthood celibacy (Ranke-Heinemann 1988) to Hindu Tantric *kuladharma*'s celebration of sexual coupling as part of religious ritual (Aho 2002), from Islamic polygamy (Poston 2004) to contemporary Mormon monogamy (Hansen 2003), from Haitian Vodou *Gede* spirit displays involving highly charged sexual language and theatrical mimicry (McAlister 2000) to Christian discomfort with masturbation (LoPresti 2003), religious orientations to various aspects of sex are drastically diverse and colorfully complex.

However, although I have gone out of my way to stress diversity and complexity in the paragraphs above, a widespread, cross-cultural study of religious regulation of sex does reveal some consistent and near–universally shared themes/teachings. First, almost every major religious tradition condemns homosexuality (Swidler 1993; Comstock and Henking 1997), generally focusing on male-male sex explicitly, with female-female sex less stigmatized or even acknowledged (Jordan 1997; Cabezon 1992; Boyarin 1993; Faure 1998). Second, almost every major religious tradition considers sex purely for the sake of pleasure as inimical to spiritual growth; that is, sex as a physically and/or emotionally satisfying goal in and of itself is seldom considered a holy or sacred endeavor. And third, sex is generally considered only acceptable and appropriate when it is practiced between a man and woman within the confines of a marital relationship.[2]

Having acknowledged that religious approaches to sex are varied, diverse, and contradictory even within the same nominal religion, and having further acknowledged that despite this diversity there are some discernible sexual regulations that most major religions do hold in common—let's get back to my friend Heather.

As you recall, Heather was having premarital sex with her boyfriend, Dil. And even though it was within the confines of a committed relationship, she still felt guilty on rainy, postcoital mornings. Since that conversation I had with Heather, I've had countless more along similar lines—most often when teaching my seminar titled "Sex and Religion." One student wrote in one of her papers that when she first had sex with her longtime boyfriend, she laid there beneath his moving body wracked with guilt, imagining visions of an extremely angry Virgin Mary hovering over the bed, condemning her to hell. Another student, during a class discussion, revealed that she always felt "dirty" after making love—even with her fiancé! She said that ever since she began having sex, she would always have to clean her bedroom, kitchen, or bathroom immediately afterward; as she only recognized later in life, the cleaning ritual served as a necessary symbolic cleansing of her own sex-soiled body. A friend recently shared with me the extended guilty turmoil he experienced as a young adolescent during his first years of masturbating and the painful embarrassment he felt each time he had to confess his masturbation to his priest.

What's with all this guilt surrounding sex? What's the big deal about masturbation? Of course, you can guess that I believe it is largely linked to what traditional Christianity has "taught" our culture about such things. Please understand that I am not arguing that Christianity is the *only* reason a young woman like Heather would feel guilty after having had premarital sex. Such a theory would be absurd. There are a multitude of factors that would need to be taken into consideration to accurately explain and understand Heather's sex guilt: her family life, her upbringing, her friendships, her past relationships, her distinct psychological makeup, and so on. All I am arguing here is that her religious identity must also be taken into account and granted some heavy causal significance. To be sure, not all Christians experience guilt after sex, but as the research mentioned earlier has found, they are indeed more likely to experience guilt after sex than the nonreligious.

Additional studies—constituting quite a large body of research—have shown that a strong, traditional, conservative Christian religiosity correlates consistently with decreased sexual activity and permissiveness (Reynolds 1994; Tanfer and Cubbins 1992; Woodroof 1985, 1986; Paxton and Turner 1978). Practicing, faithful, conservative Christians are less likely to engage in a variety of noncoital sexual activities (Samuels 1997; Mahoney 1980), are less likely to engage in or enjoy oral sex (Tavris and Sadd 1977), and are less likely to have sex before marriage (Beck, Cole, and Hammond 1991; Earle and Perricone 1986; Hammond, Cole, and Beck 1993; Kanter and Zelnik 1972). As opposed to the nonreligious, Christians are more likely to experience sexual dysfunction (Masters and Johnson 1970), wait until an older age to have sex (Davidson, Darling, and Norton 1995; Baldwin, Whiteley, and Baldwin 1992), and are more likely to condemn masturbation (Gagnon 1985; Davidson, Darling, and Norton 1995) as well as various nontraditional sexual behaviors, particularly homosexuality and premarital/extramarital sexual relations (Bainbridge 1997, 295; Hunter 1983; Herek 1988; Herek and Capitanio 1995; Scheepers, Grotenhuis, and Van Der Slik 2002; Cochran and Beeghley 1991; Miller and Olson 1988; Glenn and Weaver 1979; Bibby 1996). In the most thorough and valid study of sex ever conducted within the United States, Michael et al. (1995) found that nonreligious Americans are much more likely to think about sex more often than Christians, are more likely to have had more sex partners overall than Christians, are more likely to engage in sex for longer periods of time than Christians, and are more likely to have engaged in anal sex than Christians. In sum, decades of research have so consistently found that faithful, active Christians are less sexually permissive than the nonreligious that this observation has recently been dubbed an "empirical generalization" (Haerich 1992, 361).

What is it about Christianity that breeds such sexual reluctance? Adequately answering such a question is obviously beyond the scope of this chapter. It certainly must have something to do with the Greek philosophical roots of Christianity, which constructed a body/soul dualism in which the former was ontologically denigrated (Ranke-Heinemann 1988). It may also have something to do with the fact that Christianity is the only world religion in which the central figure of worship (Jesus) is canonically portrayed as a completely asexual being, as is the very founder of the faith (Paul). With the two most important people at the heart of Christianity being understood as asexual—and for Catholics, we can also include Mary, who is believed to have remained a virgin all her life (Hamington 1995)—given this pantheon of celibates it is understandable that sex would be considered something unfit for those seeking to emulate the truly holy. Despite marginal voices arguing otherwise, it was the reigning opinions of early Christian leaders that human sexuality was spiritually degrading; celibacy and virginity were ultimately considered more sacred states of being (Pagels 1988).

However, to say that Christianity is an "antisex" religion would be going too far. My sense is that the overwhelming majority of Christians, both clergy and laity, understand sex as a natural part of life; see, for example, Timothy and Beverly LaHaye's best-selling sex manual, *The Act of Marriage: The Beauty of Sexual Love* (1976) or the current pope's *Love and Responsibility* (Wojtyla 1994). But it is important to stress that Christians do not consider any or all sex as natural and sacred—only sex within the confines of heterosexual marriage. And if you consider traditional Catholicism, then it is only sex within the confines of heterosexual marriage with the open possibility of reproduction; remember, Catholics aren't supposed to use modern forms of birth control. So while we can't responsibly characterize

Christianity as antisex, we can reasonably characterize it as quite sexually narrow, limiting, or restrictive. And many social scientists have commented on the depth and details of this restrictiveness. The early sociologist Marriane Weber, observing the historically antagonistic relationship between Christianity and sexuality, charged that:

> In reaction against the sexual license of the late-antique cultural world, the church overemphasized the ideal of mastery of instinctive drives . . . The natural basis of the fellowship of husband and wife was relegated to the realm of the sinful, that was still admittedly allowed within marriage, but that was nevertheless even there worthy of no consecration. Remaining unmarried was esteemed the more perfect condition . . . Protestantism did again elevate marriage, as "God's work," over celibacy as "the work of man," but it too left sexual love with the stain of being an "evil desire," stemming not from God but from the devil. (quoted in Lengermann and Niebrugge-Brantley 1998, 216)

Uta Ranke-Heinemann (1988), in examining the writings of some of the most prominent Christian founding fathers (Paul, Ignatius, Jerome, Justin the Martyr, Tatian, Origen, Ambrose, Chrysostom, Augustine, and Aquinas), illustrates how they all played a distinctive part in "welding Christianity and hostility to sexual pleasure into a systematic whole" (1988, 62). The church historian James Brundage (1987, 6) argues that commonly held sex-negative attitudes and beliefs held by many in the West are largely the consequences of patristic and early medieval Christian teachings which held that "sex was a source of moral defilement, spiritual pollution, and ritual impurity; hence, the argument ran, human sexuality was something to be ashamed of because it was both a result and a source of sin." Lawrence Obsorne (1993) has discussed Christian "sexual pessimism"—the linkage of sexual love with death. In his discussion of various strands within Christianity, from Gnosticism to Catholicism, Osborne reveals the depths to which human sex can be vilified. Throughout much of Christendom, the celibate has been deemed holier and closer to God and more deserving of everlasting life than the sexually active, who has been deemed sinful and closer to Satan and death. The same with the virgin compared with the nonvirgin. The human body has been largely viewed as a corrupting entity, a thing to be ashamed of, controlled, and ultimately condemned. Again from James Brundage (1987, 8):

> Western Christendom has been more restrictive in its interdiction of sensual pleasure than most other human societies. Western Christians have commonly associated sensuality with sin, guilt, and fear of damnation . . . virtue has come to be identified with sexual abstinence [and] purity with rejection of sexuality . . . few [other religions] have carried fear of sexuality to the point of loathing and disgust, as Western Christians have done.

Given this discussion concerning Christianity's restrictive sexual regulation, it is interesting to note that where traditional Christianity is most clearly waning in the contemporary world, so too are conservative, restrictive sexual norms and values. Consider certain countries in Northwestern Europe—Iceland, Sweden, Norway, Denmark, England, Germany, the Netherlands—where traditional Christian beliefs are at an all-time low (Bruce 1999a; Trost 2000). These are also countries characterized by relative sexual permissiveness: more and more couples live together and have children out of wedlock, homosexual relations are widely accepted and often legally protected, prostitution is accepted and often legally sanctioned, premarital sex is widespread and relatively acceptable, public funding of birth control is widespread, sex education permeates the school systems, and so on. I would argue that it is no accident that the Western nations exhibiting the greatest degree of secularization are in turn the nations with the most sexually liberal cultures. A decrease in traditional Christianity in a given nominally Christian society seems to be followed by a blooming of sexual permissiveness.

Is a blooming of sexual permissiveness a good thing, or is it unhealthy and immoral? Is widespread societal acceptance of sex outside of marriage wonderful or horrible? Is societal acceptance of homosexual relations laudable or something to be condemned? Is sex education in schools a good thing or a bad thing? I don't know what your personal answers to these questions may be. But I'll predict one thing: your opinions on these matters will most likely be directly tied to your religious upbringing and current religious identity, or lack thereof.

Notes

1. Three nights later, while King was at a meeting at the First Baptist Church, his house was bombed. Luckily, his wife and daughter were not hurt.
2. There are admittedly many exceptions to these three commonly shared sexual regulations. For instance, many religions today do have thriving gay communities within their circles. And there may be religious groups somewhere out there that do see sex in and of itself as a sacred pastime, and there may also exist some religious groups that do accept and even praise sexual intimacy outside the confines of monogamous marriage (i.e., The Family/Children of God), but such deviant traditions are excruciatingly few and far between.

CONCLUSION
The Matter of Belief

"Belief, ritual, and spiritual experience," argues I. M. Lewis (1971, 11), are "the cornerstones of religion." There are certainly other significant elements to religious life, such as the importance of congregating, as discussed in the introduction, or the pervading emphasis on altruism. But for me, *belief* is of paramount concern. Religions tend to be based upon claims about the nature of this world and this reality that can be characterized as dramatically implausible or flatly unbelievable, at least from an outsider/empirical/sociological standpoint. What fascinates me is how and why these claims are believed as true by so many millions of people. Let me declare at the outset of this final chapter that I will not offer an airtight, definitive, data-driven answer. I simply hope to make a compelling case that matters of how and why people believe what they believe is a pressing topic for sociological investigation. On top of that, I will suggest that at least one of the many reasons that helps explain why people believe the flatly unbelievable is related to matters of social location (as I argued in chapter 2) and processes of social learning and social interaction (as I argued in chapter 3).

Once again, I'll draw from my own personal history to get the ball rolling:

Marni Bauer[1] was my first serious girlfriend. I was fifteen and she was sixteen. She had big, beautiful eyes and did even worse than I did on weekly French quizzes. In addition to enjoying ballet, loving the music of The Doors, and keeping score for the high school baseball team, Marni was also a born-again Christian. She was the daughter of a Baptist preacher. Despite her willingness to ditch class on occasion and drink her fair share of beer on the weekends, she attended church every Sunday. She prayed regularly. She studied her Bible. Sometimes I would ask her about her religious beliefs, which included the following:

- There was a God who resided up in Heaven and a Satan who resided down in Hell.
- God made a human woman pregnant here on Earth about two thousand years ago and the son who resulted from this pregnancy was the Savior of all humans.
- This son was killed, but then subsequently rose from the dead.
- All humans are born sinners, and unless we take this son of God into our hearts as our personal Savior, we will be tortured in burning flames for eternity after we die.

When Marni shared these beliefs with me, I was literally dumbfounded. "You *actually* believe that?" was all I could say, over and over again. I had heard these traditional Christian beliefs before, of course. But I had never actually known anyone intimately who held them to be literally true. I simply couldn't understand how Marni— a bright, fun, wonderful person—could sincerely believe what to me seemed so obviously unbelievable, bordering on the absurd. But she did, passionately so. And she believed even more than what I listed above. For instance, she believed that her father could cure people of deadly diseases merely by channeling the healing power of the Lord and directing it into the bodies of the afflicted. She also believed that nuclear weapons had been prophesied in the Bible and were undeniable indicators that the world was coming to a brutal end as foretold in the Book of Revelation, the final book of the New Testament. Her strong belief in what seemed to me to be manifestly impossible/nonsensical assertions left me puzzled, and plagued me long after she and I had broken up. Even more puzzling, as I grew older, was learning that millions of people shared Marni's beliefs and that skeptical agnostics such as myself were a distinct (and often despised) minority, at least in this country.

As one who doesn't believe the major truth claims of any religion I have ever studied, I have always found personal comfort in a simple statement that I think Carl Sagan put forth. Drawing upon David Hume (1962 [1748]; 1976 [1757]), Sagan declared the following: *Extraordinary claims require extraordinary evidence.* If someone makes a claim, especially a controversial, unique, or unusual claim, they need to offer impressive proof or evidence to back up their assertion. And the more extraordinary and unusual the claim, the more compelling (in both quality and quantity) must their evidence be.

Let me offer a quick example.

If I said to you that yesterday evening a dog ran by my house in the middle of the night, you would probably just assume I was telling the truth. Even though I can present no evidence—no dog footprints, no dog hairs, no photos, no witnesses—you'd still probably accept that what I was saying was factual. Why? Because it isn't so unusual for a dog to run past someone's house at night—in fact, it's quite common. But let's say I raised the stakes a bit. Let's say I claimed that a *pink* dog ran past my house at midnight. Pink dogs are pretty rare. It would be perfectly natural for your suspicions to be raised a little. But what if I continued to increase the extraordinariness of my claim and I said that *thirty* pink dogs ran past my house in the middle of the night. If there were no dog tracks at all, no pink hairs on my lawn, no photos, no other witnesses, no information about a circus nearby missing thirty pink dogs, it would be reasonable for you to start wondering if what I was saying was actually true or not. Even if there were dog tracks—that doesn't mean the dogs were pink, right? A little corroborating evidence concerning a certain aspect of my story does not prove the whole of it. Now what if I went even further and claimed that thirty pink dogs ran by my house at night, stopped on my front lawn, did a circular dance while singing a dirge, and then flew up and away into the night sky. For you to believe that what I was saying actually happened, you'd need a hell of a lot of evidence. Other witnesses probably wouldn't even cut it (maybe it was a mass delusion, or maybe my neighbors are lying just to get some media attention). Photos probably wouldn't cut it (they could be faked). A tape recording wouldn't sway you (someone could easily create noises that sounded like dogs singing a dirge). In short, what would be required for any reasonable person to believe that my Pink Dog Flight into the Night Sky really, actually occurred would be an entire conglomeration, a whopping array, a major arsenal of substantial, hard, and diverse evidence. Again, the more extraordinary the claim, the more extraordinary the evidence must be.

Let's forget flying pink dogs. I've never seen any nor have I ever heard of anyone else claiming to have seen any. But how about flying saucers? Millions of Americans believe in UFOs and extraterrestrials/aliens (Goode 2000, 148). Frankly, in my opinion, that's not really such a big deal. After all, there *could* be UFOs out there and there *could* be aliens out there. Even without much direct proof or impressive evidence, one could believe that they exist—somewhere out there in that vast universe or beyond. But how about if you met a man who told you that aliens not only exist but recently came to his house at night, abducted him, took him onto their spaceship, conducted violating/probing medical experiments on his body, and then plopped him back into his bed and flew away. Would you believe it? Even if the person seemed completely sincere in his claim—wouldn't you need some pretty heavy evidence to be convinced that it all really happened?

According to a 1991 Roper Poll, roughly 3.7 million Americans believe that they have been abducted by aliens (Goode 2000, 2; see also Shermer 1997). Were they? After all, either they were (or at least some of them were) or they weren't. That is, either there are actually aliens flying around in UFOs abducting Americans or there aren't. If you think these claims of abduction are true, fair enough; you don't really have anything much to explain because the situation is fairly straightforward: millions of people believe they were abducted by aliens because they were—end of story (Mack 1995). However, if you don't think that there are aliens flying around abducting Americans, then you've got a major puzzle on your hands crying out for explanation: how is it that millions of people can believe what is simply not true?

As Erich Goode (2000, 43) explains:

> If UFO's are not real, then aren't the reasons why some people say they
> have been kidnapped by aliens psychologically and sociologically inter-
> esting? Aren't the reasons why so much of the public embraces such as-
> sertions likewise interesting? . . . If these events [alien abductions]

literally and concretely happened, persons who observed them are simply reporting what they have seen. But if they didn't happen, *what caused them to believe they did?*

Precisely.

I am personally not convinced that Americans are actually being abducted by aliens. I hold this opinion not because I don't *want* to believe in alien abductions, but because the claim of alien abduction is quite an extraordinary one and, as of yet, no extraordinary proof/evidence has been provided to sufficiently convince me that the claims are true. So now here comes the challenge: being relatively secure in my disbelief in alien abductions, how do I then explain why millions of people sincerely believe that they were abducted? If I don't believe in alien abductions, I am then in the position as a social scientist of having to offer a reasonable theory as to why others do.

Consider the Aetherius Society.[2] Right here in my hometown of Claremont, California, there is a chapter of this international UFO-believing group that was founded in 1955 by George King (Rasmussen 2003). King was a London cabby and yoga master who claimed to have received hundreds of "cosmic transmissions" from "space masters." These aliens told him that he was a chosen human, charged with the mission of gathering followers and using cosmic energy transferred to him via flying saucers for healing and other ends.

Now, as a sociologist interested in studying the Aetherius Society, I have my work cut out for me. First of all, I could explore issues of race: are Aetherians predominantly of one race or another? Why? I could explore gender issues: do men or women dominate the movement? I could explore economic issues: how wealthy are the Aetherians? Where do they get their money? How do they spend their money? I could explore political issues: do they get involved in political debates? I could look into the ways in which the Aetherians affect other aspects of the social landscape: do they influence what gets taught in elementary schools? Do they participate in church basketball leagues? I could look at their group development over the decades, their recruiting techniques, their governance structure, their competition from other alien-believing groups, and so on. In short, studying and critically analyzing multiple sociological aspects of the

Aetherius Society would leave me busy for quite a long time. But aside from my examining such sociological questions, isn't the most fundamental question—the most obvious matter begging for an answer—the following: *how can these people believe this stuff?* For me, explaining how thousands of people can believe space aliens charged George King with an interplanetary mission is the most crucial puzzle.

Pink dogs, flying saucers—now let's get to what this book is all about: religion. The fact is, many religions assert various claims about the world, history, reality, life, death, and the universe that make flying pink dogs and the existence of space aliens seem quite tame and rather unremarkable by comparison. Many religions posit truth claims that are fundamentally, manifestly implausible. For instance, millions of Jews believe that thousands of years ago an all-powerful divine god capable of creating planets, moons, and suns spoke to a human, Moses. While Moses stood on the top of a tall mountain amidst thunder, lightening, smoke, and the sound of a trumpet, this god relayed to him various commandments for humans to obey, such as the injunction that anyone who curses their father or mother must be killed. The Jewish scriptures also describe Samson, who purportedly killed one thousand men with the jawbone of a donkey. And then there's Elijah, who supposedly flew up into heaven in the company of a floating chariot drawn by horses made of fire; he also raised people from the dead.

Millions of Muslims believe that one night in the seventh century, in Mecca, Saudi Arabia, a human, Muhammad, was visited by an angel, Gabriel. This angel placed Muhammad on a flying horse which transported him to the city of Jerusalem, where he was greeted by Abraham, Moses, Jesus, and a group of other prophets. Following this gathering, he and Gabriel climbed a ladder up into the seven levels of heaven (Armstrong 1992). Lawgiving gods amidst lightning and thunder, angels, flying horses, ladders to heaven, airborne chariots with horses of fire, lethal jawbones, raising people from the dead— just scratching the surface of two major world religions (Judaism and Islam), one immediately comes across an array of extraordinary claims that lack even a minuscule amount of solid evidence.

Consider—for a final example—a little bit of the background behind the birth of the Mormon religion. In 1826, while in his early twenties, Joseph Smith Jr. got into some trouble with the law. He was arrested in the town of Bainbridge, New York, and brought before a court for an official hearing, charged with engaging in a confidence scheme/con game (Persuitte 2000). Prior to his arrest, Smith had claimed that he had a special ability to find buried treasure. He said that he had a magical rock and that when he put this magical rock into his hat, it gave him the miraculous power to be able to see deep into the earth and locate buried treasure. One man, Simpson Sowel, believed Smith, and paid him money for his special powers. Smith told Sowel where to dig, but when the treasure failed to materialize, Smith said that some spell kept causing the treasure to move elsewhere within the earth. This went on for some time until concerned relatives of Sowel called the authorities. After a court hearing and the giving of testimony (including Smith's own admission that he did claim to use a magic stone for the sake of finding buried treasure), Joseph Smith was found responsible for deceiving and swindling his clients (Sowel wasn't his only victim). The justice of the peace who ran the hearing concluded that Smith was a "disorderly person and an imposter." Rather than face possible jail time, Smith fled the county before a full trial could take place.

A couple of years later, with his buried-treasure scheme no longer workable, Smith delved into the business of founding a major world religion—the Church of Jesus Christ of Latter-day Saints, now popularly known as the Mormons.[3] He claimed that he was visited by angels, and that one angel in particular, Moroni, told him about the existence of a set of golden plates buried in the earth near his home in upstate New York—plates supposedly containing sacred scriptures. Smith then claimed that he dug out the plates and put them in a secured trunk. He said that if he or anyone else looked directly at the golden plates, their eyes would be damaged. However, by employing the help of two magic stones, which granted him some sort of x-ray vision, Smith claimed to be able to see through the trunk and read the writing on the plates, allowing him to translate them from "reformed Egyptian" to English. In April of 1828 Smith began reading what was supposedly on these plates to a friend, Martin Harris, who served as his scribe. So here's how it worked: the two men sat in a room, divided by a sheet which ran between the two of them, and with his x-ray-vision-granting stones, Smith would "see" the golden plates through the trunk and dictate what he was claiming to be reading/translating. Harris wrote down what Smith dictated for two months—over a hundred pages' worth.

But then came trouble: Harris' wife, Lucy, stole the manuscript. She thought Smith was a con man and didn't believe any of his claims. She challenged Smith to do it all over again: start at the beginning and reread out loud to her husband those hundred pages from those golden plates and then she'd compare the stolen pages in her possession to the new ones Smith would again speak aloud. If they matched up, she'd believe Smith was actually reading from golden plates. If they didn't match up, she'd know it was a hoax. David Persuitte (2000, 79) explains how Joseph Smith got out of this dilemma:

> In July . . . Joseph declared that he had received his first "revelation" from the "Lord." This revelation "chastised" him for losing the 116 pages and revoked his translation "privileges" for a "season" (which perhaps indicates that Joseph Smith needed time to work out his new plans). In a subsequent revelation, the Lord commanded Joseph not to retranslate the same section of the plates that he had translated before. By the design of Satan (Joseph had the Lord say), those who had taken the pages would alter them to keep the work from being accepted. Instead, Joseph was to translate from the plates of Nephi, which were a different section of the plates, but which contained a more detailed account of the same things he had previously translated.

And so he did. The result was the eventual publication of the Book of Mormon. The golden plates soon went up into heaven. Joseph Smith continued to claim to be visited by angels, and for many years he claimed to have had hundreds of direct communications with a divine creator god. Today, there are over eleven million Mormons, and their numbers grow stronger every year. Angels, gods, golden plates, magic seeing stones, x-ray vision—extraordinary claims lacking equally extraordinary evidence, and yet believed to be true by millions.

If Joseph Smith really was visited by angles, really did talk with God, and really did translate sacred scriptures from golden plates, then sociologists of religion should simply stick to what they do best:

examining issues of race, class, gender, sexuality, recruitment techniques, media relations, political activity, and so on, in relation to the Mormon religion. But if Joseph Smith's claims are false—and lacking extraordinary evidence, we must conclude that they are—we have a lot of explaining to do: why are so many of our fellow humans convinced?

I could go on and on, laying out some of the more fantastical claims of Scientologists, Sikhs, Catholics, Hindus, Buddhists, Jains, Swedenborgians, Sufis, Pentecostals—but the point should be clear: probing the beliefs of most religions will immediately reveal an endless array of mind-boggling, implausible, and extraordinary truth claims that lack compatible extraordinary evidence. And yet every single one of those implausible claims is sincerely believed as true by thousands—and in most cases millions—of people. And that is precisely what makes religions distinct from other social collectives: they are often based upon and centered around a body of explicitly extraordinary and often fantastical truth claims. This is what makes religions so remarkably and uniquely interesting: their members sincerely believe the manifestly unbelievable. Thus, I am always slightly miffed when my fellow social scientists of religion declare that we cannot discuss, approach, or theorize about the truth or falsity of religious beliefs (see pages 31–32). For me, it is my fellow human beings' very honest, sincere, and proud acceptance of unbelievable, fantastical, and unreasonable claims that makes religion a compelling topic for penetrating analysis and inquiry. Understanding why and how people can believe the manifestly unbelievable is the very reason why I got into this discipline.

To be sure, every religion has its more liberal, nonliteralist members. There are many contemporary Christians who don't take the Bible as the literal, direct word of God. There exists a significant proportion of Muslims who don't take the Qur'an as the literal, direct word of God. There are many Mormons who do not take the Book of Mormon as the literal, direct word of God. Certainly most Jews don't take the Bible as the direct, literal word of God. Within every major religion there are those who find meaning in the metaphorical, the implicit. They value their religion for the good works it inspires, the beauty of its traditions, the sense of meaning and identity it provides, the comfort it offers, the ethics and morals is sustains, and they are able to interpret various beliefs, claims, dogmas, details, teachings, scriptures, and directives in their own personally meaningful, imaginative, liberal, allegorical, aesthetic, nonliteral ways.

However, there are millions of religious people who *do* take their religion as being literally true: they believe that the prophet of their faith did a have a direct and real communication with the Creator of All Existence, that their holy scriptures are the direct, literal word of God, that specific miracles did actually occur, that laws and rules laid down by religious authorities or in scriptures are undeniably and eternally true, that accounts for the origins of life and earth are factually correct, and so on. If you are not such a believer, then you must be curious as to—and desire to explain—why so many millions of your fellow human beings are.

The bottom line is that for sociologists of religion the truth or falsity of religious beliefs should not—*cannot*—be avoided, because explaining how millions of sound, reasonable people can believe the manifestly unbelievable is an unavoidable dilemma for the social scientist. As Steve Bruce (1999a, 36) rightly posits, if people believe "what is evidently false or clearly resistant to proof, we need to provide a causal story saying how this could happen."

Most devoutly religious people can easily explain why they believe that which lacks evidence or is resistant to proof: their belief simply isn't based on "evidence" or "proof." Their belief is not based on empirically observable data. Their belief is something mystical, transcendent, heartfelt (like love), and beyond the limited methods of hard science. Every deeply religious individual that I have ever discussed these matters with—when pushed on sticky, bizarre, or incredibly hard to explain specifics about their religion—invariably proclaims that it all boils down to faith. And such an admission generally ends the conversation; how can one argue with that?

However, most of the nonreligious people I know just don't get the whole "faith" thing and see it as a sort of cop-out to fall back on when one can't prove one's beliefs (Barker, 1992). Such religiously tone-deaf individuals tend to just throw up their hands and say of the devoutly religious: "They are crazy." After conversations with Mormon missionaries or Jehovah's Witnesses or fervently religious aunts and uncles, most secular people I know just write the devoutly religious off as being nuts. However, even a cursory investigation into religion—even a minor amount of hands-on study among the religious— will quickly reveal that religious people are not insane or crazy. Far from it. They are intelligent, sound, thoughtful, inquisitive, rational, normal people (at least as intelligent, sound, thoughtful, inquisitive, rational, and normal as are the nonreligious). Writing religious believers off as crazy is to live in denial concerning the bulk of humanity; such a conclusion simply isn't supported by any substantial or convincing data/evidence. In fact, there is some evidence suggesting that religious people are actually of sounder mind than the nonreligious (Francis and Kaldor 2002; Schumaker 1992; Stark and Bainbridge 1996; Crawford, Handal, and Weiner 1989)!

If not simplistically dismissing the fervently religious as nuts, most nonbelievers will then offer distinctly psychological theories to explain religious belief: people believe that which isn't true because it makes them feel better, it provides comfort and security, it offers simplistic answers to complex dilemmas, it gives them hope, it makes them feel loved, it offers emotional solace in the face of death, and so on (see, for example, Weber 1963; Freud 1961 [1927]; Greeley 1982; Stark and Bainbridge 1985; Shermer 2000, 1997; Fromm 1955; Hinde 1999; Goodenough 1965; Clark 1958; Spinks 1963). Such psychological theories of religious belief offer a great deal of explanatory insight. Without question, the specific beliefs of successful religions speak to people's unconscious and deep-seated needs, wishes, fears, and desires. However, to stop at the individual/psychological level always limits our understanding of human behavior, as Émile Durkheim (1982 [1895], 1951) so forcefully argued. In the words of Clifford Geertz (1973, 99), without culture, an individual human would be "functionally incomplete . . . a kind of formless monster with neither sense of direction nor power of self-control, a chaos of spasmodic impulses and vague emotions." Religion cannot simply be reduced to individual, psychological processes, needs, or dispositions—little if anything about human life can. We are social animals and there can exist no individual psychology apart from social inter-action. Thus, for a full-bodied account of why people are religious, we need to incorporate the sociological perspective.

A sociological approach to explaining religion is one that is ever cognizant of the socially constructed nature of nearly all human endeavors; it is an approach that always employs a critical, debunking orientation, even when approaching religion. The sociological approach to religion stresses the external constraints on individual religious choices, such as those related to time and place. The sociological approach to religion also emphasizes processes of socialization and social learning by exposing the deep influence family, friends, spouses, and significant others have on determining individual religiosity. Sociologists of religion are always aware of the ways in which various aspects of the social environment influence and shape religion and, conversely, how religion can be a determining factor in affecting the larger social world. And finally—coming back to the subject of belief—I would suggest that a sociological approach to religion would highlight the ways in which people may often believe things—even the most miraculous, fantastical, irrational, and implausible things—simply because others in their social world do (recall chapter 3). In the words of Stark and Finke (2000, 117), "social networks make religious beliefs plausible."

Consider my daughter, Ruby, and her friend, Katie. Ruby is four years old. For the first three years of her life Katie was her best friend. But then last year Katie moved to Chicago. Ruby was heartbroken. Last month, my wife took Ruby to visit Katie for a few days. One afternoon, my wife overheard a conversation between the two girls as they were trying to figure out what game of make-believe to play.

"Let's play fairies," Ruby suggested. "I'll be Queen Mab and you can be a princess fairy."

"No," replied Katie. "I don't want to play that. I don't like fairies."

"C'mon . . . it'll be fun."

"No. How about we play Jesus," suggested Katie.

"What's that?" asked Ruby.

"I'll be baby Jesus and you be his mama."

"I don't know that movie."

"Well Jesus was this man and he got killed and really bloody."

"That sounds yucky."

"But then he came back to life and went to Heaven and he will be up there when we die."

"Hm . . . well all I know is that in my house my parents say '*Jesus Crimeny!*' when they get mad."

"What does that mean?"

"I don't know. Can't we just play fairies?"

Right now, at age four, my daughter Ruby believes in fairies. She thinks they exist for the simple reason that we told her that they exist. We have told her countless stories about fairies, we have read her countless books with drawings and pictures full of fairies, and she has even seen movies with very realistic-looking fairies flying all around. Sometimes at night she will sit at her window sill and sing out to them, earnestly beseeching them to pay her a visit.

Right now, Katie believes in Jesus. She thinks that he lived long ago, died a bloody death, and then came back to life and flew to Heaven where he lives with God and angels. She thinks this is all true for the simple reason that her parents told her it was true. Her teachers and priest at Sunday school have told her about Jesus. They have read her many books and shown her many drawings and pictures depicting his story. She may have even seen a movie or two about him. Sometimes at night she earnestly prays to him up in heaven.

I have a prediction: Ruby's belief in fairies won't last much longer—maybe a year or two, at most. But Katie's belief in Jesus will probably last her a lifetime. Why the difference? Why will a belief in fairies be nearly impossible for Ruby to sustain, but a belief in Jesus be relatively easy for Katie to sustain? Of course, if one is a Bible-believing Christian, then the answer is obvious: it is simply a matter of true belief versus false belief; fairies simply don't really exist, but a resurrected Jesus really is up in heaven—case closed. But if one isn't a Bible-believing Christian, such an answer is unsatisfactory. There's something else going on concerning Ruby's imminent loss of belief in fairies and Katie's probable sustained belief in a risen Jesus.

All psychological matters aside, as a sociologist, I predict that Ruby will most likely lose her faith in fairies because as she gets older, she will find fewer and fewer people sharing and supporting such a belief. At some point, she will even lose me and her mother as fairy-believing allies; eventually we will have to admit to her that we don't really believe in them. However, Katie will find plenty of social support for her belief in Jesus—and not just any social support, but social support from the most important people in her life: her parents, grandparents, cousins, aunts, uncles, and so on. Depending on where she goes to school, she'll find her belief further supported by teachers and friends. And additionally, she will be repeatedly told that empirical proof of Jesus isn't even necessary, that she need only have "faith" in order to believe.

Of course, it is very possible that Katie will lose her faith in Jesus one day. And I suppose it is also hypothetically possible that Ruby will maintain her belief in fairies until she dies. But I sincerely doubt that either will happen. And I don't think that Katie's sustained faith in Jesus or Ruby's loss of faith in fairies will have much to do with genetic, bioevolutionary predispositions for certain types of belief, or psychological needs for comfort and security, or scientific experimentation, or rational decision making. I think that the most salient and significant factor in determining their future beliefs will be social interactions with others.

Of course, a theory emphasizing social interaction and socialization as explanatory factors of religious belief has its obvious limitations, and can only go so far. First of all, not everyone accepts the beliefs of their parents, friends, neighbors, or community; there are always deviants who believe things totally at odds with those of significance in their social world (recall John Walker Lindh). Though such "belief deviants" are unusual, they are present in every group, which means that while socializing processes explain many people's religiosity, they don't explain everyone's, everywhere, all the time. Second, socialization and social learning of religion don't explain religion's origins—how did it start in the first place?[4] And, third, if people simply believed what others around them believed, there would never be any change or development. And this clearly isn't the case: religions come and go throughout the course of history, traditions transform, beliefs gain and lose popularity, and some societies dramatically become more or less religious over the course of generations. For example, if people simply believed what their parents and neighbors believed, we could not account for the growth of Christianity and Islam with the simultaneous decline of pagan traditions. If belief were strictly a matter of social mimicry, we would never see the dramatically low levels of Christian belief and religious involvement that we currently find in various countries in Western Europe, which have experienced observable secularization (Bruce 2001, 1999a; Shand 1998; Houtman and Mascini 2002). So how do we explain such dramatic and far-reaching changes in belief among populations over time? Like all aspects of human behavior, surely the acquisition and loss of certain beliefs is a complicated mix of social, psychological, political, cultural, economic, and genetic processes mysteriously working themselves out in an infinite number of directions and degrees. Sociology does not have all the answers when it comes to religion. No discipline does. But it does offer many revealing and provocative insights which greatly illuminate our understanding of that most intriguing aspect of human belief and behavior called religion.

Notes

1. Not her real name.
2. See www.Aetherius.org for more information.
3. Many scholars erroneously cite the beginning of Smith's special religious calling as occurring in 1820, when he was fourteen and supposedly experienced his first visit by angels one day in the woods. This famous visit by angels, however, is never written or spoken about until the 1840s, some twenty years after the supposed event, casting serious doubt upon its historical veracity (Persuitte 2000).
4. Many scholars of religion have offered theories on how religion arose, that is, the very origin or genesis of religion. However, such theories— though often compelling and provocative—are inherently futile (Goode 1951). Religion began so long ago, in so many diverse environments and in such diverse manifestations, that no theory of how religion began can ever be supported by a compelling body of evidence. I agree with Ronald Johnstone (1997, 21) that "any evidence of an origin or origins [of religion] has been lost in prehistory . . . such evidence, if it ever existed, is lost in antiquity . . . any hypothesis regarding religion's origins is doomed to remain forever tentative."

BIBLIOGRAPHY

Aho, James. 2002. *The Orifice as Sacrificial Site: Culture, Organization, and the Body.* New York: Aldine de Gruyter.

Aidala, A. 1985. "Social Change, Gender Roles, and New Religious Movements." *Sociological Analysis* 46: 287–314.

Alba, R. 1990. *Ethnic Identity.* New Haven: Yale University Press.

Aldridge, Alan. 2000. *Religion in the Contemporary World.* Cambridge, England: Polity Press.

Argyle, M., and B. Beit-Hallahmi. 1975. *The Social Psychology of Religion.* London: Routledge and Kegan Paul.

Armstrong, Karen. 1992. *Muhammad: A Biography of the Prophet.* New York: HarperCollins.

Baer, Hans. 1998. "African American Religious Experience." In *Encyclopedia of Religion and Society* edited by William Swatos. Walnut Creek, Calif.: Alta Mira Press.

Bahr, Howard, and Stan Albrecht. 1989. "Strangers Once More: Patterns of Disaffiliation from Mormonism." *Journal for the Scientific Study of Religion* 28 (2): 180–200.

Baile, David. 1992. *Eros and the Jews: From Biblical Israel to Contemporary America.* New York: Basic Books.

Bainbridge, William Sims. 1978. *Satan's Power: A Deviant Psychotherapy Cult.* Berkeley: University of California Press.

———. 1997. *The Sociology of Religious Movements.* New York: Routledge.

Baldwin, John, Scott Whiteley, and Janice Baldwin. 1992. "The Effect of Ethnic Group on Sexual Activities Related to Contraception and STDs." *Journal of Sex Research* 29 (2): 189–205.

Baldwin, Lewis. 1991. *There Is a Balm in Gilead: The Cultural Roots of Martin Luther King, Jr.* Minneapolis: Fortress Press.

Balmer, R. 1994. "American Fundamentalism: The Ideal Femininity." in *Fundamentalism and Gender*, edited by J. S. Hawley, 47–62. New York: Oxford University Press.

Barker, Dan. 1992. *Losing Faith in Faith: From Preacher to Atheist.* Madison, WI: Freedom From Religion Foundation, Inc.

Barker, Eileen. 1984. *The Making of a Moonie: Choice or Brainwashing?* New York: Basil Blackwell.

Batson, C. Daniel, Patricia Schoenrade, and W. Larry Ventis. 1993. *Religion and the Individual: A Social-Psychological Perspective.* New York: Oxford University Press.

Beaman, Lori. 1999. *Shared Beliefs, Different Lives: Women's Identities in Evangelical Context.* St. Louis: Chalice Press.

Beck, Scott, Bettie Cole, and Judith Hammond. 1991. "Religious Heritage and Premarital Sex: Evidence From a National Sample of Young Adults." *Journal for the Scientific Study of Religion* 30 (2): 173–180.

Becker, Howard. 1963. *Outsiders: Studies in the Sociology of Deviance.* New York: The Free Press.

Bengston, V. L. 1975. "Generation and Family Effects in Value Socialization." *American Sociological Review* 40: 358–371.

Bennion, Janet. 1998. *Women of Principle: Female Networking in Contemporary Mormon Polygyny.* New York: Oxford University Press.

Benson, Peter, Michael Donahue, and Joseph Erickson. 1989. "Adolescence and Religion: A Review of the Literature from 1970 to 1986." *Research in the Scientific Study of Religion* 1: 153–181.

Berger, Peter. 1961. *The Precarious Vision.* Garden City, N.Y.: Doubleday and Company.

———. 1963. *Invitation to Sociology.* New York: Anchor Books.

———. 1967. *The Sacred Canopy.* New York: Anchor Books.

———. 1970. *A Rumor of Angels.* New York: Anchor Books.

———. 1979. *The Heretical Imperative.* Garden City, N.Y.: Anchor Press.

———. 1999. *The Descularization of the World: Resurgent Religion and World Politics.* Grand Rapids, Mich.: William B. Eerdmans Publishing Company.

———2001. "Reflections on the Sociology of Religion Today." *Sociology of Religion* 62 (4): 443–454.

Biale, Rachel. 1984. *Women and Jewish Law.* New York: Schocken Books.

Bibby, Reginald. 1996. "Sex and the Single Parishioner." Paper presented at the annual meeting of the Society for the Scientific Study of Religion, Nashville, Tenn.

Bibby, Reginald, and Merlin Brinkerhoff. 1973. "The Circulation of Saints: A Study of People Who Join Conservative Churches." *Journal for the Scientific Study of Religion* 12: 273–283.

Billingsley, Andrew. 1998. *Mighty Like a River: The Black Church and Social Reform.* New York: Oxford University Press.

Bird, Frederick. 1993. "Charisma and Leadership in New Religious Movements." In *Religion and the Social Order: The Handbook on Cults and Sects in America*, edited by David Bromley and Jeffrey Hadden. Greenwich, Conn.: JAI Press.

Bowden, Henry. 1981. Foreword to *Saints, Slaves, and Blacks: The Changing Place of Black People within Mormonism*, by Newell Bringhurst. Westport, Conn.: CTL Greenwood Press.

Boyarin, Daniel. 1993. *Carnal Israel.* Berkeley: University of California Press.

Brasher, B. 1998. *Godly Women.* New Brunswick, N.J.: Rutgers University Press.

Bringhurst, Newell. 1981. *Saints, Slaves, and Blacks: The Changing Place of Black People within Mormonism.* Westport, Conn.: Greenwood Press.

Brink, William, and Louis Harris. 1963. *The Negro Revolution in America.* New York: Simon and Schuster.

Bromley, David, and Jeffrey Hadden. 1993. "Exploring the Significance of Cults and Sects in America: Perspectives, Issues, and Agendas." In *Religion and the Social Order: The Handbook on Cults and Sects in America,* edited by David Bromley and Jeffrey Hadden. Greenwich, Conn.: JAI Press.

Bromley, David, and James Richardson, eds. 1983. *The Brainwashing/Deprogramming Controversy: Sociological, Psychological, Legal, and Historical Perspectives.* New York: Edwin Mellen.

Brown, K. M. 1991. *Mama Lola: A Vodou Priestess in Brooklyn.* Berkeley: University of California Press.

———. 1994. "Fundamentalism and the control of women." In *Fundamentalism and Gender,* edited by J. S. Hawley, 175–201. New York: Oxford University Press.

Bruce, Steve, ed. 1992. *Religion and Modernization: Sociologists and Historians Debate the Secularization Thesis.* Oxford: Oxford University Press.

———. 1993. "Religion and Rational Choice: A Critique of Economic Explanations of Religious Behavior." *Sociology of Religion* 54 (2): 193–205

———. 1996. *Religion in the Modern World: From Cathedrals to Cults.* Oxford: Oxford University Press.

———. 1999a. *Choice and Religion: A Critique of Rational Choice.* Oxford: Oxford University Press.

———. 1999b. *Sociology: A Very Short Introduction.* Oxford: Oxford University Press.

———. 2001. "Christianity in Britain, R.I.P." *Sociology of Religion* 62 (2): 191–203.

Brundage, James. 1987. *Law, Sex, and Christian Society in Medieval Europe.* Chicago: University of Chicago Press.

Bryant, Joseph. 2000. "Cost-Benefit Accounting and the Piety Business: Is Homo Religiosus, at Bottom, Homo Economicus?" *Method and Theory in the Study of Religion* 12 (4): 520–548.

Bush, Lester, and Armand Mauss. 1984. *Neither White Nor Black: Mormon Scholars Encounter the Race Issue in a Universal Church.* Salt Lake City: Signature Books.

Byrnes, Joseph. 1984. *The Psychology of Religion.* New York: The Free Press.

Cabezon, Jose Ignaacio. 1992. *Buddhism, Sexuality, and Gender.* Albany: State University of New York Press.

Caldwell, Sarah. 1999. *Oh Terrifying Mother: Sexuality, Violence, and Worship of the Goddess Kali.* New York: Oxford University Press.

Candland, Douglas. 1993. *Feral Children and Clever Animals.* New York, Oxford University Press.

Castelli, Elizabeth. 2001. *Women, Gender, and Religion: A Reader.* New York: Palgrave.

Chalfant, Paul, Robert Beckley, and Eddie Palmer. 1994. *Religion in Contemporary Society.* Itasca, Ill.: F. E. Peacock Publishers, Inc.

Chalfant, Paul, and Emily LeBeff. 1991. *Understanding People and Social Life.* St. Paul: West Publishing.

Chaves, Mark. 1995. "On the Rational Choice Approach to Religion." *Journal for the Scientific Study of Religion* 34: 98–104.

———. 1997. *Ordaining Women: Culture and Conflict in Religious Organizations.* Cambridge: Harvard University Press.

Clark, Walter Huston. 1958. *The Psychology of Religion.* New York: Macmillan.

Cochran, John, and Leonard Beeghley. 1991. "The Influence of Religion on Attitudes toward Nonmarital Sexuality: A Preliminary Assessment of Reference Group Theory." *Journal for the Scientific Study of Religion* 30 (1): 45–62.

Collins, Randal. 1992. *Sociological Insight: An Introduction to Non-Obvious Sociology.* New York: Oxford University Press.

Comstock, Gary David, and Susan Henking. 1997. *Que(e)rying Religion.* New York: Continuum.

Cornwall, Marie. 1988. "The Influence of Three Agents of Religious Socialization: Family, Church, and Peers." In *The Religion and Family Connection: Social Science Perspectives,* edited by Darwin Thomas. Provo, Utah: Religious Studies Center, Brigham Young University.

Covington, Dennis. 1995. *Salvation on Sand Mountain: Snake Handling and Redemption in Southern Appalachia.* Cambridge, Mass.: Perseus Publishing.

Crawford, Mark, Paul Handal, and Richard Weiner. 1989. "The Relationship between Religion and Mental Health/Distress." *Review of Religious Research* 31 (1): 16–26.

Daly, Mary. 1968. *The Church and the Second Sex.* New York: Harper and Row.

Daugherty, L. R., and J. M. Burger. 1984. "The Influence of Parents, Church, and Peers on the Sexual Attitudes and Behaviors of College Students." *Archives of Sexual Behavior* 13: 351–359.

Davidson, Kenneth, Carol Anderson Darling, and Laura Norton. 1995. "Religiosity and the Sexuality of Women: Sexual Behavior and Sexual Satisfaction Revisited." *Journal of Sex Research* 32 (3): 235–243.

Davie, Grace. 1999. "Europe: The Exception That Proves the Rule?" In *The Desecularization of the World,* edited by Peter Berger. Grand Rapids, Mich.: William B. Eerdmans Publishing Company.

Davis, C. F. 1989. *The Evidential Force of Religious Experience.* Oxford: Clarendon Press.

Davis, Stephen. 1993. *Risen Indeed: Making Sense of the Resurrection.* Grand Rapids, Mich.: William B. Eerdmans Publishing Company.

Davis, Townsend. 1998. *Weary Feet, Rested Souls: A Guided History of the Civil Rights Movement.* New York: W. W. Norton and Company.

Delameter, J. D. 1989. "The Social Control of Human Sexuality." In *Human Sexuality: The Societal and Interpersonal Context,* edited by K. McKinney and S. Specher, 30–62. Norwood, N.J.: Ablex Publishing Company.

D'Emilio, John, and Estelle Freedman. 1988. *Intimate Matters: A History of Sexuality in America.* New York: Harper and Row.

Denison, Barbara. 1998. "Sexuality and Fertility." In *Encyclopedia of Religion and Society,* edited by William Swatos. Walnut Creek, Calif.: Alta Mira Press.

Dick, Anthony. 1990. "Religious Movements and Brainwashing Litigation: Evaluation Key Testimony." In *In Gods We Trust: New Patterns of Religious Pluralism in America*, edited by T. Robbins and D. Anthony. New Brunswick: N.J.: Transaction.

Doherty, Earl. 2000. *The Jesus Puzzle*. Ottawa, Canada: Canadian Humanist Publications.

———. 2001. *Challenging the Verdict: A Cross-Examination of Lee Strobel's "The Case for Christ."* Ottawa: Age of Reason Publications.

Du Bois, W. E. B. 1989 [1903]. *The Souls of Black Folk*. New York: Bantam Books.

———. 2003 [1903]. *The Negro Church*. Walnut Creek, Calif.: Alta Mira Press.

Dudley, R. L. 1996. "How Seventh Day Adventist Lay Members View Women Pastors." *Review of Religious Research* 38 (2): 133–145.

Dudley, R. L., and M. G. Dudley. 1986. "Transmission of Religious Values from Parents to Adolescents." *Review of Religious Research* 28: 3–15.

Durkheim, Émile. 1915. *The Elementary Forms of the Religious Life*. New York: The Free Press.

———. 1951. *Suicide: A Study in Sociology*. New York: The Free Press.

———. 1982 [1895]. *The Rules of Sociological Method*. New York: The Free Press.

Earle, John, and Philip Perricone. 1986. "Premarital Sexuality: A Ten-Year Study of Attitudes and Behavior on a Small University Campus." *Journal of Sex Research* 22 (3): 304–310.

Ebaugh, Helen Rose. 2002. "Return of the Sacred: Reintegrating Religion in the Social Sciences." *Journal for the Scientific Study of Religion* 41 (3): 385–395.

Eck, Diana. 2001. *A New Religious America: How a "Christian Country" Has Become the World's Most Religiously Diverse Nation*. New York: Harper-Collins.

Eitzen, Stanley, and Maxine Baca Zinn. 2001. *In Conflict and Order: Understanding Society*. Boston: Allyn and Bacon.

Ellegard, Alvar. 1999. *Jesus: One Hundred Years before Christ*. Woodstock, N.Y.: Overlook Press.

Embry, Jessie. 1994. *Black Saints in a White Church: Contemporary African American Mormons*. Salt Lake City: Signature Books.

Emerson, Michael, and Christian Smith. 2000. *Divided by Faith: Evangelical Religion and the Problem of Race in America*. New York, NY: Oxford University Press.

Erickson, J. A. 1992. Adolescent Religious Development and Commitment: A Structural Equation Model of the Role of Family, Peer Group, and Educational Influences. *Journal for the Scientific Study of Religion* 31: 131–152.

Fairclough, Adam. 1987. *To Redeem the Soul of America: The Southern Christian Leadership Conference and Martin Luther King, Jr.* Athens: University of Georgia Press.

Faure, Bernard. 1998. *The Red Thread: Buddhist Approaches to Sexuality*. Princeton, N.J.: Princeton University Press.

Feuerbach, Ludwig. 1989 [1841]. *The Essence of Christianity*. Amherst, N.Y.: Prometheus Books.

Finke, Roger, and Rodney Stark. 1992. *The Churching of America 1776–1990*. New Brunswick, N.J.: Rutgers University Press.

Finney, J. M. 1978. "A Theory of Religious Commitment." *Sociological Analysis* 39: 19–35.

Fletcher, Richard. 1997. *The Barbarian Conversion: From Paganism to Christianity*. New York: Henry Holt and Company.

Foster, Lawrence. 1984. *Religion and Sexuality: The Shakers, the Mormons, and the Oneida Community*. Urbana: University of Illinois Press.

Fowlkes, M. A. 1988. "Religion and Socialization." In *Handbook of Preschool Religious Education*, edited by D. Ratcliff. Birmingham, Ala.: Religious Education Press.

Francis, Leslie, and Lawrence Brown. 1991. "The Influence of Home, Church, and School Prayer among 16-Year-Old Adolescents in England." *Review of Religious Research* 33: 112–122.

Francis, Leslie, and Peter Caldor. 2002. "The Relationship between Psychological Well-Being and Christian Faith and Practice in an Australian Population Sample." *Journal for the Scientific Study of Religion* 41 (1): 179–184.

Fraser, David, and Campolo, Tony. 1992. *Sociology through the Eyes of Faith*. New York: HarperCollins.

Frederick, C. Harris. 1999. *Something Within: Religion in African-American Political Activism*. New York: Oxford University Press.

Fredrickson, George. 1995. *Black Liberation*. New York: Oxford University Press.

Freke, Timothy, and Peter Gandy. 1999. *The Jesus Mysteries*. New York: Harmony Books.

Freud, Sigmund. 1961 [1927]. *The Future of an Illusion*. New York: W. W. Norton.

———. 1994 [1930]. *Civilization and Its Discontents*. New York: Dover Publications.

Fromm, Erich. 1955. *The Dogma of Christ and Other Essays on Religion, Psychoanalysis, and Culture*. New York: Henry Holt and Company.

Fuller, Robert. 2001. *Spiritual, but Not Religious: Understanding Unchurched America*. New York: Oxford University Press.

Gaede, Stan. 1976. "A Causal Model of Belief-Orthodoxy: Proposal and Empirical Test." *Sociological Analysis* 37: 205–217.

Gagnon, John. 1985. "Attitudes and Responses of Parents to Pre-Adolescent Masturbation." *Archives of Sexual Behavior* 14 (5): 451–466.

Gallup, George, Jr. 1997. *Public Opinion*. Wilmington, Del.: Scholarly Resources.

Gallup, George, Jr., and D. Michael Lindsay. 1999. *Surveying the Religious Landscape*. Harrisburg, Pa.: Morehouse Publishing.

Garfinkel, Hardol. 1967. *Studies in Ethnomethodology*. Englewood Cliffs, N.J.: Prentice Hall.

Geertz, Clifford. 1973. *The Interpretation of Cultures*. New York: Basic Books.

Gerth, Hans, and C. Wright Mills. 1946. *From Max Weber: Essays in Sociology*. New York: Oxford University Press.

Gesell, Arnold. 1940. *Wolf Child and Human Child*. New York: Harper and Brothers Publishers.

Gil, Vincente. 1990. "Sexual Fantasy Experiences and Guilt among Conservative Christians: An Exploratory Study." *Journal of Sex Research* 27 (4): 629–638.

Gilman, Charlotte Perkins. 1923. *His Religion & Hers* New York: Century.

Glassner, Barry. 1999. *The Culture of Fear.* New York: Basic Books.

Glenn, Norval, and Charles Weaver. 1979. "Attitudes toward Premarital, Extramarital, and Homosexual Relations in the U.S. in the 1970s." *Journal of Sex Research* 15 (2): 108–118.

Goffman, Erving. 1959. *The Presentation of Self in Everyday Life.* New York: Anchor Books.

Goldberg, Robert. 1991. *Grassroots Resistance: Social Movements in Twentieth Century America.* Belmont, Calif.: Wadsworth.

Goldman, Marion. 1999. *Passionate Journeys: Why Successful Women Joined a Cult.* Ann Arbor: University of Michigan Press.

Goode, Erich. 2000. *Paranormal Beliefs: A Sociological Introduction.* Prospect Heights, Ill.: Waveland Press.

———. 2002. *Deviance in Everyday Life.* Prospect Heights, Ill.: Waveland Press.

Goode, William. 1951. *Religion Among The Primitives.* New York: The Free Press.

Goodenough, Erwin. 1965. *The Psychology of Religious Experiences.* New York: Basic Books.

Greeley, Andrew. 1975. *The Sociology of the Paranormal: A Reconnaissance.* Beverly Hills, Calif.: Sage Publications.

———. *Religion: A Secular Theory.* 1982. New York: The Free Press.

———. 1991. "American Exceptionalism: The Religious Phenomenon." In *Is America Different? A New Look at American Exceptionalism,* edited by Byron Shafer. Oxford: Clarendon Press.

———. 1995. *Sociology and Religion.* New York: HarperCollins.

Greeley, Andrew, and Michael Hout. 1999. "Americans' Increasing Beliefs in Life after Death: Religious Competition and Acculturation." *American Sociological Review* 64: 813–835.

Gross, Rita. 1996. *Feminism and Religion: An Introduction.* Boston: Beacon Press.

Grotenhuis, Manfred, and Peer Scheepers. 2001. "Churches in Dutch: Causes of Religious Disaffiliation in the Netherlands, 1937–1995." *Journal for the Scientific Study of Religion* 40 (4): 591–606.

Grover, Mark. 1990. "The Mormon Priesthood Revelation and the São Paulo, Brazil Temple." *Dialogue: A Journal of Mormon Thought* 23 (spring): 39–53.

Guardia, Ricardo Fernandez. 1913. *The History of the Discovery and Conquest of Costa Rica.* New York: Thomas Y. Crowell Company.

Gunnoe, Marjorie, and Kristin Moore. 2002. "Predictors of Religiosity among Youth Aged 17–22: A Longitudinal Study of the National Survey of Children." *Journal for the Scientific Study of Religion* 41 (4): 613–622.

Guthrie, Stewart. 1993. *Faces in the Clouds: A New Theory of Religion.* New York: Oxford University Press.

Hacker, Andrew. 1995. *Two Nations: Black and White, Separate, Hostile, and Unequal.* New York: Ballantine Books.

Haddad, Y. Y., and J. L. Esposito, eds. 1998. *Islam, Gender, and Social Change.* New York: Oxford University Press.

Haddad, Y. Y., and E. B. Findly. 1985. *Women, Religion, and Social Change.* Albany: State University of New York Press.

Hadaway, Kirk, and Mark Chaves. 1993. "What the Polls Don't Show: A Closer Look at US Church Attendance." *American Sociological Review* 58: 741–752.

Hadaway, Kirk, and Penny Long Marler. 1993. "All in the Family: Religious Mobility in America." *Review of Religious Research* 35 (2): 97–111.

Haerich, Paul. 1992. "Premarital Sexual Permissiveness and Religious Orientation: A Preliminary Investigation." *Journal for the Scientific Study of Religion* 31 (3): 361–365.

Hak, Durk. 1998. "Rational Choice Theory." In *Encyclopedia of Religion and Society*, edited by William Swatos. Walnut Creek, Calif.: Alta Mira Press.

Hamilton, Malcolm. 1995. *The Sociology of Religion: Theoretical and Comparative Perspectives.* New York: Routledge.

Hamington, Maurice. 1995. *Hail Mary?* New York: Routledge.

Hammond, Judith, Bettie Cole, and Scott Beck. 1993. "Religious Heritage and Teenage Marriage." *Review of Religious Research* 35 (2): 117–133.

Hammond, Phillip, and David Machacek. 1993. "Cults and Sects in America: Organizational Development." In *Religion and the Social Order: The Handbook on Cults and Sects in America*, edited by David Bromley and Jeffrey Hadden. Greenwich, Conn.: JAI Press.

Hansen, Klaus. 1981. *Mormonism and the American Experience.* Chicago: University of Chicago Press.

———. 2003. "Mormonism and Sex." In *Sex and Religion*, edited by Christel Manning and Phil Zuckerman. Belmont, Calif.: Wadsworth.

Hardy, B. C. 1992. *Solemn Covenant.* Urbana: University of Illinois Press.

Hartman, Keith. 1996. *Congregations in Conflict: The Battle over Homosexuality.* New Brunswick, N.J.: Rutgers University Press.

Hayes, B., and Y. Pittelkow. 1993. "Religious Belief, Transmission, and the Family." *Journal of Marriage and the Family* 55: 755–766.

Haywood, C. L. 1983. "Women's Authority in Spiritualist groups." *Journal for the Scientific Study of Religion* 22: 157–166.

Helms, Randel. 1988. *Gospel Fictions.* Amherst, N.Y.: Prometheus Books.

Herberg, Will. 1955. *Protestant Catholic Jew.* Garden City, N.Y.: Anchor Books.

Herek, Gregory. 1988. "Heterosexuals' Attitudes toward Lesbians and Gay Men: Correlates and Gender Differences." *Journal of Sex Research* 25 (4): 451–477.

Herek, Gergory, and John Capitanio. 1995. "Black Heterosexuals' Attitudes toward Lesbians and Gay Men in the United States." *Journal of Sex Research*, 32 (2): 95–105.

Herold, Edward, and Leslie Way. 1983. "Oral-Genital Sexual Behavior in a Sample of University Females." *Journal of Sex Research* 19 (4): 327–338.

Hinde, Robert. 1999. *Why God Persists: A Scientific Approach to Religion.* New York: Routledge.

Hoge, Dean. 1981. *Converts, Dropouts, Returnees: A Study of Religious Change among Catholics.* New York: Pilgrim.

Hoge, Dean, Benton Johnson, and Donald Luidens. 1994. *Vanishing Boundaries: The Religion of Mainline Protestant Baby Boomers*. Louisville, Ky.: Westminster/John Knox Press.

Hoge, D., G. Petrillo, and E. Smith. 1978. "Determinants of Church Participation and Attitudes among High School Youth." *Journal for the Scientific Study of Religion* 17: 359–379.

———. 1982. "Transmission of Religious and Social Values from Parents to Teenage Children." *Journal of Marriage and the Family* 44: 569–580.

Hoodfar, Homa. 1997. "The Veil in Their Minds and on Our Heads: Veiling Practices and Muslim Women." In *The Politics of Culture in the Shadow of Capital*, edited by L. Lowe and D. Lloyd, 248–279. Durham, N.C.: Duke University Press.

hooks, bell. 1984. *Feminist Theory: From Margin to Center*. Boston: South End Press.

Hout, M., and A. Greeley. 1987. "The Center Doesn't Hold: Church Attendance in the United States, 1940–1984." *American Sociological Review* 52: 325–345.

Houtman, Dick, and Peter Mascini. 2002. "Why Do Churches Become Empty, While New Age Grows? Secularization and Religious Change in the Netherlands." *Journal for the Scientific Study of Religion* 41 (3): 455–473.

Hume, David. 1962 [1748]. *Inquiry concerning Human Understanding*. New York: Macmillan.

———. 1976 [1757]. *The Natural History of Religion*. Oxford: Clarendon Press.

Hunsberger, Bruce, and L. B. Brown. 1984. "Religious Socialization, Apostasy, and the Impact of Family Background." *Journal for the Scientific Study of Religion* 23 (3): 239–251.

Hunter, James D. 1983. *American Evangelicalism: Conservative Religion and the Quandary of Modernity*. New Brunswick, N.J.: Rutgers University Press.

Hyde, Kenneth. 1990. *Religion in Childhood and Adolescence: A Comprehensive Review of the Research*. Birmingham, Ala.: Religious Education Press.

Iadarola, A. 1985. "The American Catholic Bishops and Woman: From the Nineteenth Amendment to the ERA." In *Women, Religion, and Social Change*, edited by Y. Y. Haddad and E. B. Findly, 457–476. Albany: State University of New York Press.

Iannaccone, L. 1992. "Religious Markets and the Economics of Religion." *Social Compass* 39: 123–131.

———. 1995. "Voodoo Economics? Reviewing the Rational Choice Approach to Religion." *Journal for the Scientific Study of Religion* 34: 76–88.

Isaacson, Lynne. 1995. "Rule Making and Rule Breaking in a Jesus Community." In *Religion and the Social Order*, edited by David Bromley, Mary Jo Neitz, and Marion Goldman, 5: 181–201.

Ivins, Stanley. 1972. "Notes on Mormon Polygamy." In *Mormonism and American Culture*, edited by Marvin Hill and James Allen. New York: Harper and Row.

Jacobs, J. 1989. *Divine Disenchantment*. Bloomington: Indiana University Press.

———. 1991. "Gender and Power in New Religious Movements." *Religion* 21: 345–356.

James, William. 1936 [1902]. *The Varieties of Religious Experience*. New York: Modern Library.

Johnson, Benton. 1963. "On Church and Sect." *American Sociological Review* 28: 539–549.

———. 1971. "Church and Sect Revisited." *Journal for the Scientific Study of Religion* 10: 124–137.

———. 1977. "Sociological Theory and Religious Truth." *Sociological Analysis* 38 4: 368–388.

———. 1992. "On Founders and Followers: Some Factors in the Development of New Religious Movements." *Sociological Analysis* 53: 1–13.

Johnstone, Ronald. 1997. *Religion in Society: A Sociology of Religion*. Upper Saddle River, N.J.: Prentice Hall.

Jordan, Mark. 1997. *The Invention of Sodomy in Christian Theology*. Chicago: University of Chicago Press.

Joseph, N. B. 1992. "Mehitzah: Halakhic Decisions and Political Consequences." In *Daughters of the King: Women and the Synagogue*, edited by S. Grossman and R. Haut. Philadelphia: The Jewish Publication Society.

Juergensmeyer, Mark. 2001. *Terror in the Mind of God: The Global Rise of Religious Violence*. Berkeley: University of California Press.

Jung, P. B., M. E. Hunt, and R. Balakrishnan. *Good Sex: Feminist Perspectives from the World's Religions*. New Brunswick, N.J.: Rutgers University Press.

Juschka. Darlene, ed. 2001. *Feminism in the Study of Religion*. London and New York: Continuum.

Kalish, R. A., and A. I. Johnson. 1972. "Value Similarities and Differences in Three Generations of Women." *Journal of Marriage and the Family* 34: 49–54.

Kanagy, Conrad, and Donald Kraybill. 1999. *The Riddles of Human Society*. Thousand Oaks, Calif.: Pine Forge Press.

Kanter, J. F., and M. Zelnik. 1972. "Sexual Experience of Young Unmarried Women in the United States." *Family Planning Perspectives* 4: 9–18.

Kaplan, Mordechai. 1981 [1934]. *Judaism as a Civilization*. Philadelphia: The Jewish Publication Society of America Reconstructionist Press.

Kappeler, Victor, Mark Blumberg, and Gary Potter. 2000. *The Mythology of Crime and Criminal Justice*. Prospect Heights, Ill.: Waveland Press.

Kedem, Peri. 1995. "Dimensions of Jewish Religiosity." In *Israeli Judiasm*, edited by Shlomo Deshen, Charles Liebman, and Moshe Shokeid. New Brunswick, N.J.: Transaction Publishers.

Kelley, James. 1997. *Skeptic in the House of God*. New Brunswick, N.J.: Rutgers University Press.

Kelley, Jonathan, and Nan Dirk De Graaf. 1997. "National Context, Parental Socialization, and Religious Belief: Results from 15 Nations." *American Sociological Review* 62 (August): 639–659.

Kimball, Edward, ed. 1982. *The Teachings of Spencer W. Kimball*. Salt Lake City: Bookcraft.

King, Martin Luther, Jr. 1963. *Strength to Love*. New York: Harper and Row.

————. 1998. *The Autobiography of Martin Luther King, Jr.* New York: Warner Books.

Kinsey, Alfred, et. al. 1948. *Sexual Behavior in the Human Male.* Philadelphia: W. B. Saunders Company.

Kleugel, James. 1980. "Denominational Mobility." *Journal for the Scientific Study of Religion* 19: 26–39.

Kniss, Fred. 1996. "Ideas and Symbols as Resources in Intra-Religious Conflict: The Case of American Mennonites." *Sociology of Religion* 57 (1): 7–23.

Kosmin, Barry, and Seymour Lachman. 1993. *One Nation under God: Religion in Contemporary American Society.* New York: Crown Publishers.

Kox, Willem, Wim Meeus, and Harm t'Hart. 1991. "Religious Conversion of Adolescents: Testing the Lofland and Stark Model of Religious Conversion." *Sociological Analysis* 52: 227–240.

Kramer, Laura. 2001. *The Sociology of Gender: A Brief Introduction.* Los Angeles: Roxbury Publishing Company.

Kristof, Nicholas. 2003. "God, Satan, & the Media." *New York Times,* March 4, section A. p. 25.

Kurtz, Lester. 1995. *Gods in the Global Village.* Thousand Oaks, Calif.: Pine Forge Press.

La Barre, Weston. 1970. *The Ghost Dance: Origins of Religion.* Garden City, N.Y.: Doubleday.

Ladd, Kevin, and Bernard Spilka. 2002. "Inward, Outward, and Upward: Cognitive Aspects of Prayer." *Journal for the Scientific Study of Religion* 41 (3): 475–484.

LaHaye, Tim, and Beverly LaHaye. 1976. *The Act of Marriage: The Beauty of Sexual Love.* Grand Rapids, Mich.: Zondervan.

Leatham. Miguel. 1997. "Rethinking Religious Decision-Making in Peasant Millenarianism: The Case of Nueva Jeruslen." *Journal of Contemporary Religion* 12: 295–309.

Leidner, Harold. 1999. *The Fabrication of the Christ Myth.* Tampa, Fla.: Survey Books.

Lemert, Charles. 2002. *Social Things: An Introduction to the Sociological Life.* Lanham, Md.: Rowman and Littlefield.

Lengermann, Particia Madoo, and Jill Niebrugge-Brantley. 1998. *The Women Founders: Sociology and Social Theory 1830–1930.* New York: McGraw-Hill.

Lenski, G. 1963. *The Religious Factor.* Garden City, N.Y.: Doubleday.

Levy, Peter. 1998. *The Civil Rights Movement.* Westport, Conn.: Greenwood Press.

Lewis, I. M. 1971. *Ecstatic Religion: An Anthropological Study of Spirit Possession and Shamanism.* Baltimore, Md.: Penguin Books.

Lincoln, Eric. 1984. *Race, Religion, and the Continuing American Dilemma.* New York: Hill and Wang.

Livermore, Harold. 1958. *A History of Spain.* New York: Grove Press.

Lobdell, William, and Larry Stammmer. 2002. "Mormon Scientist, Church Clash over DNA Test." *Los Angeles Times,* December 8, A21.

Lofland, John. 1966. *Doomsday Cult: A Study of Conversion, Proselytization, and Maintenance of Faith.* Englewood Cliffs, N.J.: Prentice Hall.

Lofland, John, and Rodney Stark. 1965. "Becoming a World-Saver": A Theory of Conversion to a Deviant Perspective." *American Sociological Review* 30: 862–875.

LoPresti, Anthony. 2003. "Christianity and Sex." In *Sex and Religion*, edited by Christel Manning and Phil Zuckerman. Belmont, Calif.: Wadsworth.

MacDonald, Dennis. 2000. *The Homeric Epics and the Gospel of Mark*. New Haven: Yale University Press.

Mack, John. 1995. *Abductions: Human Encounters with Aliens*. New York: Bantam Books.

Mahoney, E. R. 1980. "Religiosity and Sexual Behavior among Heterosexual College Students." *Journal of Sex Research* 16 (1): 97–113.

Malinowski, Bronislaw. 1954. *Magic, Science, and Religion*. Garden City, N.Y.: Doubleday Anchor Books.

Manning, Christel. 1999. *God Gave Us the Right: Conservative Catholic, Evangelical Protestant, and Orthodox Jewish Women Grapple with Feminism*. New Brunswick, N.J.: Rutgers University Press.

Manning, Christel, and Phil Zuckerman. 2004. *Sex and Religion*. Belmont, Calif.: Wadsworth Publishing.

Manolache, A. 1990. "Orthodoxy and Women: A Romanian Perspective." In *Women, Religion, and Sexuality*, edited by J. Becher, 172–183. Philadelphia: Trinity Press International.

Marger, Martin. 2002. *Social Inequality: Patterns and Processes*. New York: McGraw-Hill.

Marler, Penny Long, and Kirk Hadaway. 2002. " 'Being Religious' or 'Being Spiritual' in America: A Zero-Sum Proposition? *Journal for the Scientific Study of Religion* 41 (2): 289–300.

Marsh, Charles. 1999. *God's Long Summer: Stories of Faith and Civil Rights*. Princeton: Princeton University Press.

Massey, Douglas, and Nancy Denton. 1993. *American Apartheid: Segregation and the Making of the Underclass*. Cambridge: Harvard University Press.

Masters, W. H., and V. Johnson. 1970. *Human Sexual Inadequacy*. Boston: Little, Brown.

Mauss, Armand. 1994. *The Angel & The beehive: The Mormon Struggle with Assimilation*. Urbana: U. of Illinois Press.

McAdam, Doug. 1988. *Freedom Summer*. New York: Oxford University Press.

McAlister, Elizabeth. 2000. "Love, Sex, and Gender Embodied: The Spirits of Haitian Vodou." In *Love, Sex, and Gender in the World Religions*, edited by Joseph Runzo and Nancy Martin. Oxford: Oneworld.

McCutcheon, Russell. 2001. *Critics Not Caretakers: Redescribing the Public Study of Religion*. Albany: State University of New York Press.

McCutcheon, Russell, ed. 1999. *The Insider/Outsider Problem in the Study of Religion*. London: Cassell.

McGuire, Meredith. 1997. *Religion: The Social Context*. Belmont, Calif.: Wadsworth Publishing Company.

Michael, Robert, John Gagnon, Edward Laumann, and Gina Kolata. 1995. *Sex in America: A Definitive Survey*. New York: Warner Books.

Miller, Brent, and Terrance Olson. 1988. "Sexual Attitudes and Behavior of High School Students in Relation to Background and Contextual Factors." *Journal of Sex Research* 24: 194–200.

Miller, Timothy, ed. 1991. *When Prophets Die: The Postcharismatic Fate of New Religious Movements.* Albany: State University of New York Press.

Mills, C. Wright. 1959. *The Sociological Imagination.* New York: Oxford University Press.

Mills, Edgar. 1983. "The Sociology of Religion as an ASA Subdiscipline." *Sociological Analysis* 44 (4): 339–354.

Moaddel, Mansoor. 1998. "Religion and Women: Islamic Modernism versus Fundamentalism." *Journal for the Scientific Study of Religion* 37 (1): 108–130.

Moore, Laurence. 1986. *Religious Outsiders and the Making of Americans.* New York: Oxford University Press.

Morris, Aldon. 1984. *The Origins of the Civil Rights Movement: Black Communities Organizing for Change.* New York: The Free Press.

Moses, Wilson Jeremiah. 1993. *Black Messiahs and Uncle Toms: Social and Literary Manipulations of a Religious Myth.* University Park: Pennsylvania State University Press.

Mosley, R. J., and K. Brockenbrough. 1988. "Faith Development in the Preschool Years." In *Handbook of Preschool Religious Education,* edited by D. Ratcliff. Birmingham, Ala.: Religious Education Press.

Musick, Marc, and John Wilson. 1995. "Religious Switching for Marriage Reasons." *Sociology of Religion* 56 (3): 257–270.

Myers, Scott. 1996. "An Interactive Model of Religiosity Inheritance: The Importance of Family Context." *American Sociological Review* 61 (October): 858–866.

Nelsen, Hart. 1981. "Gender Differences in the Effects of Parental Discord on Preadolescent Religiousness." *Journal for the Scientific Study of Religion* 20: 351–360.

O'Brien, Joanne, and Martin Palmer. 1993. *The State of Religion Atlas.* New York: Simon and Schuster.

Osborne, Lawrence. 1993. *The Poisoned Embrace.* New York: Pantheon Books.

Otto, Rudolph. 1952 [1917]. *The Idea of the Holy.* London: Oxford University Press.

Ozorak, E. W. 1989. "Social and Cognitive Influences on the Development of Religious Beliefs and Commitment in Adolescence." *Journal for the Scientific Study of Religion* 28: 448–463.

Padover, Saul, ed. 1974. *Karl Marx on Religion.* New York: McGraw-Hill Book Company.

Pagels, Elaine. 1988. *Adam, Eve, and the Serpent.* New York: Vintage Books.

Palm, Irving, and Jan Trost. 2000. "Family and Religion in Sweden." In *Family, Religion, and Social Change in Diverse Societies,* edited by Sharon Houseknecht and Jerry Pankhurst. New York: Oxford University Press.

Park, Chris. 1994. *Sacred Worlds: An Introduction to Geography and Religion.* New York: Routledge.

Parrinder, Geoffrey. 1996. *Sexual Morality in the World's Religions.* Oxford: Oneworld Publications.

Paxton, Anne Lee, and Edward Turner. 1978. "Self-Actualization and Sexual Permissiveness, Satisfaction, Prudishness, and Drive among Female Undergraduates." *Journal of Sex Research* 14 (2): 65–80.

Perlinger, C., ed. 1992. *Episcopalian Women*. New York: Oxford University Press.

Persinger, Michael. 1987. *Neuropsychological Bases of God Beliefs*. New York: Praeger.

Persuitte, David. 2000. *Joseph Smith and the Origins of the Book of Mormon*. Jefferson, N.C.: McFarland and Company.

Peterson, J. A. 1964. *Education for Marriage*. New York: Scribner's.

Plaskow, Judith. 1990. *Standing Again at Sinai: Judaism from a Feminist Perspective*. San Francisco: HarperCollins.

Poston, Larry. 2004. "Sexuality in Islam." In *Sex and Religion*, edited by Christel Manning and Phil Zuckerman. Belmont, Calif.: Wadsworth.

Potvin, Raymond, and C. F. Lee. 1982. "Adolescent Religion: A Developmental Approach." *Sociological Analysis* 43 (2): 131–144.

Potvin, R. H., and D. M. Sloane. 1985. "Parental Control, Age, and Religious Practice." *Review of Religious Research* 27: 3–14.

Price, Robert. 1999. "Of Myth and Men." *Free Inquiry* 20 (1): 24–36.

———. 2000. *Deconstructing Jesus*. Amherts, N.Y.: Prometheus Books.

Putnam, Robert. 2000. *Bowling Alone: The Collapse and Revival of American Community*. New York: Simon and Schuster.

Raboteau, Albert. 1999. *Canaan Land: A Religious History of African Americans*. New York: Oxford University Press.

Raboteau, Albert. 1978. *Slave Religion: The "Invisible Institution" & The Antebellum South*. New York: Oxford University Press.

Raines, Howell. 1977. *My Soul Is Rested: The Story of the Civil Rights Movement in the Deep South*. New York: Penguin Books.

Ranke-Heinemann, Uta. 1988. *Eunuchs for Heaven: The Catholic Church and Sexuality*. London: Andre Deutsch.

Rasmussen, Celia. 2003. "Flying Saucer Society Sought Peak Experience on Baldy." *Los Angeles Times*, January 12, B4.

Reynolds, Dynette Ivie. 1994. "Religious Influence and Premarital Sexual Experience: Critical Observations on the Validity of a Relationship." *Journal for the Scientific Study of Religion* 33 (4): 382–387.

Richardson, James. 1993a. "A Social Psychological Critique of 'Brainwashing' Claims about Recruitment to New Religions." *Religion and the Social Order* 3B: 75–97.

———. 1993b. "Definitions of Cult: From Socioligical-Technical to Popular-Negative." *Review of Religious Research* 34: 348–356.

Richardson, James, and Massion Introvigne. 2001. "'Brainwashing' Theories in European Parlimentary and Administrative Reports on 'Cults' and 'Sects.'" *Journal for the Scientific Study of Religion* 40: 143–168.

Richardson, James, and Mary Stewart. 1977. "Conversion Process Models and the Jesus Movement." *American Behavioral Scientist* 20: 819–838.

Richardson, James, and Barend van Driel. 1997. "Journalists' Attitudes toward New Religious Movements." *Review of Religious Research* 39 (2): 116–128.

Richardson, John. 1998. *The Romans in Spain.* Oxford: Blackwell Publishers.

Riesebrodt, Martin. 1978. *Slave Religion: The "Invisible Institution" in the Antebellum South.* New York: Oxford University Press.

———. 1993. *Pious Passion: The Emergence of Modern Fundamentalism in the United States and Iran.* Berkeley, Calif.: University of California Press.

———. 1995. *A Fire in the Bones: Reflections on African-American Religious History.* Boston: Beacon Press.

Robbins, Thomas. 1984. "Constructing Cultist 'Mind Control.'" *Sociological Analysis* 45 (3): 241–256.

Robbins, Thomas, Dick Anthony, and Thomas Curtis. 1973. "The Limits of Symbolic Realism: Problems of Empathetic Field Observation in a Sectarian Context." *Journal for the Scientific Study of Religion* 12: 259–271.

Roberts, M. K., and J. D. Davidson. 1984. "The Nature and Source of Religious Involvement." *Review of Religious Research* 25: 334–350.

Roof, Wade Clark, and William McKinney. 1987. *American Mainline Religion.* New Brunswick, N.J.: Rutgers University Press.

Rourke, Mary. 1998. "Redefining Religion in America." *Los Angeles Times,* June 21, A1.

Ruane, Janet, and Karen Cerulo. 2000. *Second Thoughts: Seeing Conventional Wisdom through the Sociological Eye.* Thousand Oaks, Calif.: Pine Forge Press.

Ruether, Rosemary Radford. 1983. *Sexism and God-Talk.* Boston: Beacon Press.

Runzo, Joseph, and Nancy Martin. 2000. *Love, Sex, and Gender in the World Religions.* Oxford: Oneworld Publications.

Rustin, Bayard. 1963. *Strategies for Freedom: The Changing Patterns of Black Protest.* New York: Columbia University Press.

Samuels, Herbert. 1997. "The Relationship among Selected Demographics and Conventional and Unconventional Sexual Behaviors among Black and White Heterosexual Men." *Journal of Sex Research* 34 (1): 85–92.

Scharf, Betty. 1970. *The Sociological Study of Religion.* London: Hutchinson University Library.

Scheepers, Peer, Manfred Te Grotenhuis, and Frans Van Der Slik. 2002. "Education, Religiosity, and Moral Attitudes: Explaining Cross-National Effect Differences." *Sociology of Religion* 63 (2): 157–176.

Schumaker, J. F., ed. 1992. *Religion and Mental Health.* New York: Oxford University Press.

Schwalbe, Michael. 2001. *The Sociologically Examined Life.* Mountain View, Calif.: Mayfield Publishing Company.

Scimecca, Joseph. 1995. *Society and Freedom.* Chicago: Nelson-Hall Publishers.

Sered, Susan. 1992. *Women as Ritual Experts: The Religious Life of Elderly Jewish Women in Jerusalem.* New York: Oxford University Press.

———. 1997. "Women and Religious Change in Israel: Rebellion or Revolution. *Sociology of Religion* 58: 1–24.

Shand, Jack. 1998. "The Decline of Traditional Christian Beliefs in Germany." *Sociology of Religion* 59 (2): 179–184.

Sharot, Stephen. 2002. "Beyond Christianity: A Critique of Rational Choice Theory of Religion from a Weberian and Comparative Religions Perspective." *Sociology of Religion* 63: 427–454.

Sherkat, Darren. 1993. "Theory and Method in Religious Mobility Research." *Social Scientific Research* 22: 208–227.

Sherkat, Darren, and John Wilson. 1995. "Preferences, Constraints, and Choices in Religious Markets: An Examination of Religious Switching and Apostasy." *Social Forces* 73: 993–1026.

Shermer, Michael. 2000. *How We Believe.* New York: W. H. Freeman & Company.

———. 1997. *Why People Believe Weird Things: Pseudoscience, Superstition, and Other Confusions of Our Time.* New York: W. H. Freeman and Company.

Simmel, Georg. 1950. *The Sociology of Georg Simmel,* edited by Kurt Wolff. New York: The Free Press.

Smith, H. Shelton. 1972. *In His Image, but . . . Racism in Southern Religion 1780–1910.* Durham, N.C.: Duke University Press.

Smith, Tom. 2002. "Religious Diversity in America: The Emergence of Muslims, Buddhists, Hindus, and Others." *Journal for the Scientific Study of Religion* 41 (3): 577–585.

Snow, David, and R. Machalek. 1984. "The Sociology of Conversion." *Annual Review of Sociology* 10: 167–190.

Spickard, James. 1998. "Rethinking Religious Action: What Is 'Rational' about Rational Choice Theory?" *Sociology of Religion* 59 (2): 99–115.

Spilka, Bernard, Ralph Hood, and Richard Gorsuch. 1985. *The Psychology of Religion: An Empirical Approach.* Engelewood Cliffs, N.J.: Prentice Hall.

Spinks, George. 1963. *Psychology and Religion.* Boston: Beacon Press.

Sponberg, Ala. 2004. "Spirituality, Sexuality, and Gender in Buddhism." In *Sex and Religion,* edited by Christel Manning and Phil Zuckerman. Belmont, Calif.: Wadsworth.

Stanton, William. 1951. *The Leopard's Spots: Scientific Attitudes toward Race in America, 1815–59.* Chicago: University of Chicago Press.

Stark, Rodney. 1984. "Religion and Conformity. Reaffirming a Sociology of Religion." *Sociological Analysis* 45: 273–282.

———. 1987. "How New Religions Succeed: A Theoretical Model." In *The Future of New Religious Movements,* edited by David Bromley and Phillip Hammond, 11–29. Macon, Ga.: Mercer University Press.

———. 1996a. *The Rise of Christianity.* Princeton: Princeton University Press.

———. 1996b. "So Far So Good: A Brief Assessment of Mormon Membership Projections." *Review of Religious Research* 38 (2): 175–181.

———. 1999. "A Theory of Revelations," *Journal for the Scientific Study of Religion* 38 (2): 287–308.

———. 2000. "Secularization: R.I.P." In *The Secularization Debate,* edited by William Swatos and Daniel Olson. Lanham, Md.: Rowman and Littlefield.

Stark, Rodney, and William Sims Bainbridge. 1985. *The Future of Religion: Secularization, Revival, and Cult Formation.* Berkeley: University of California Press.

———. 1996. *Religion, Deviance, and Social Control.* New York: Routledge.

Stark, Rodney, and Roger Finke. 1993. "A Rational Approach to the History of American Cults and Sects." In *Religion and the Social Order: The*

Handbook on Cults and Sects in America, edited by David Bromley and Jeffrey Hadden. Greenwich, Conn.: JAI Press.

———. 2000. *Acts of Faith*. Berkeley: University of California Press.

Stark, Rodney, and Charles Glock. 1968. *American Piety*. Berkeley: University of California Press.

Stewart, M. W., J. T. Richardson, and R. B. Simmonds. 1976. "Life Style: Courtship, Marriage, and Family in a Changing Jesus Movement Organization." *International Review of Modern Society* 6: 155–172.

Stott, Gerald. 1988. "Familial Influence on Religious Involvement." In *The Religion and Family Connection: Social Science Perspectives*, edited by Darwin Thomas. Provo, Utah: Religious Studies Center, Brigham Young University.

Swatos, William. 1981. "Church-Sect and Cult: Bringing Mysticism Back In." *Sociological Analysis* 42: 17–26.

———, ed. 1994. *Gender and Religion*. New Brunswick, N.J.: Transaction Publishers.

Swatos, William, and Daniel Olson. 2000. *The Secularization Debate*. Lanham, Md.: Rowman and Littlefield.

Swidler, Arlene, ed. 1993. *Homosexuality and the World Religions*. Valley Forge, Pa.: Trinity Press International.

Taggart, Stephen, 1970. *Mormonism's Negro Policy: Social and Historical Origins*. Salt Lake City: University of Utah Press.

Tanfer, Koray, and Lisa Cubbins. 1992. "Coital Frequency among Single Women: Normative Constraints and Situational Opportunities." *Journal of Sex Research* 29 (2): 221–250.

Tannahill, Reay. 1980. *Sex in History*. New York: Stein and Day.

Tavris, C., and S. Sadd. 1977. *The Redbook Report on Female Sexuality*. New York: Delacorte Press.

Thalheimer, Fred. 1973. "Religiosity and Secularization in the Academic Professions." *Sociology of Education* 46: 183–202.

Thompson, Daniel. 1963. *The Negro Leadership Class*. Engelwood Cliffs, N.J.: Prentice Hall.

Thrower, James. 1999. *Religion: The Classical Theories*. Washington, D.C.: Georgetown University Press.

Troeltsch, Ernst. 1931. *The Social Teaching of the Christian Churches*. New York: Macmillan.

Trost, Jan. 2000. "Family and Religion in Sweden." In *Family, Religion, and Social Change in Diverse Societies*, edited by Sharon Houseknecht and Jerry Pankurst. New York: Oxford University Press.

Turner, Bryan. 1993. *Religion and Social Theory*. London: SAGE Publications.

Verweij, Johan, Peter Ester, and Rein Natua. 1997. "Secularization as an Economic and Cultural Phenomenon: A Cross-National Analysis." *Journal for the Scientific Study of Religion* 36 (2): 309–324.

Wallace, R. 1993. "The Social Construction of a New Leadership Role: Catholic Women Pastors." *Sociology of Religion* 54: 31–42.

Wallis, Roy. 1977. *The Road to Total Freedom: A Sociological Analysis of Scientology*. New York: Columbia University Press.

Washington, Booker T., and W. E. B. Du Bois. 1970 [1907]. *The Negro in the South*. New York: The Citadel Press.

Watling, Tony. 2002. " 'Leadership' or 'Dialogue'? Women, Authority and Religious Change in a Netherlands Community." *Sociology of Religion* 63: 515–538.

Weber, Max. 1946. *From Max Weber: Essays in Sociology*, edited by Hans Gerth and C. Wright Mills. New York: Oxford University Press.

———. 1963. *The Sociology of Religion*. Boston: Beacon.

———. 1978 [1922] *Economy and Society*. Berkeley: University of California Press.

———. 2002 [1904]. *The Protestant Ethic and the Spirit of Capitalism*. Los Angeles: Roxbury Publishing Company.

Weinberg, Meyer. 1970. *W. E. B. Du Bois: A Reader*. New York: Harper and Row.

Weis, D. L. 1983. "Affective Reactions of Women to Their Initial Experience of Coitus." *Journal of Sex Research* 19: 209–237.

Wells, G. A. 1975. *Did Jesus Exist?* London: Pemberton.

———. 1988. *The Historical Evidence for Jesus*. Buffalo, N.Y.: Prometheus Books.

Wertheimer, Jack. 1993. *A People Divided*. New York: Basic Books.

Wessinger, Catherine. 2000. *How the Millennium Comes Violently*. New York: Seven Bridges Press.

Williams, Miriam. 1998. *Heaven's Harlots: My Fifteen Years in a Sex Cult*. New York: Eagle Brook/William Morrow and Company.

Willis, Evan. 1996. *The Sociological Quest*. New Brunswick, N.J.: Rutgers University Press.

Willits, Fern, and Donald Crider. 1989. "Church Attendance and Traditional Beliefs in Adolescence and Young Adulthood: A Panel Study." *Review of Religious Research* 31 (1): 68–81.

Wilson, Bryan. 1982. *Religion in Sociological Perspective*. Oxford: Oxford University Press.

———. 1987. "Factors in the Failure of New Religious Movements." In *The Future of New Religious Movements*, edited by David Bromley and Phillip Hammond, 30–35. Macon, Ga.: Mercer University Press.

———. 1993. "Historical Lessons in the Study of Sects and Cults." In *Religion and the Social Order: The Handbook on Cults and Sects in America*, edited by David Bromley and Jeffrey Hadden. Greenwich, Conn.: JAI Press.

Wojtlya, Karel. 1994. *Love and Responsibility*. San Francisco: Ignatius Press.

Wolff, Kurt, ed. 1950. *The Sociology of Georg Simmel*. New York: The Free Press.

Woodroof, J. T. 1985. "Premarital Sexual Behavior and Religious Adolescents." *Journal for the Scientific Study of Religion* 24 (4): 343–366.

———. 1986. "Reference Groups, Religiosity and Premarital Sexual Behavior." *Journal for the Scientific Study of Religion* 25: 436–460.

Wuthnow, Robert. 1989. *The Struggle for America's Soul: Evangelicals, Liberals, and Secularism*. Grand Rapids, Mich.: William B. Eerdmans Publishing Company.

Wyatt, Gail, and Kristi Dunn. 1991. "Examining Predictors of Sex Guilt in Multiethnic Samples of Women." *Archives of Sexual Behavior* 20 (5): 471–485.

X, Malcolm. 1964. *The Autobiography of Malcolm X*. New York: Grove Press.

Yamane, D., and Polzer, M. 1994. "Ways of Seeing Ecstasy in Modern Society." *Sociology of Religion* 55: 1–25.

Yip, Andrew. 2002. "The Persistence of Faith among Nonheterosexual Christians: Evidence for the Neosecularization Thesis of Religious Transformation." *Journal for the Scientific Study of Religion* 41 (2): 199–212.

Young, Lawrence, ed. 1997. *Rational Choice Theory and Religion*. New York: Routledge.

Zablocki, Benjamin, and Thomas Robbins, eds. 2001. *Misunderstanding Cults: Searching for Objectivity in a Controversial Field*. Toronto: University of Toronto Press.

Zinnbauer, Brian, Kenneth Pargament, et al. 1997. "Religion and Spirituality: Unfuzzying the Fuzzy." *Journal for the Scientific Study of Religion* 36: 549–564.

Zuckerman, Phil. 1997. "Gender Regulation as a Source of Religious Schism." *Sociology of Religion* 58 (4): 353–373.

———. 1999. *Strife in the Sanctuary: Religious Schism in a Jewish Community*. Walnut Creek, Calif.: Alta Mira Press.

———. ed. 2000. *Du Bois on Religion*. Walnut Creek, Calif.: Alta Mira Press.

———. 2002. "The Sociology of Religion of W. E. B. Du Bois." *Sociology of Religion* 63 (2): 239–253.

INDEX